Essays by
"The Free Republican,"
1784–1786

Essays by
"The Free Republican,"
1784-1786

BENJAMIN LINCOLN, JR.

Edited and with an Introduction by

PHILIP C. MEAD & GORDON S. WOOD

LIBERTY FUND

Indianapolis

Introduction, editorial matter, and index © 2016 by Liberty Fund, Inc.

Cover art: Thomas Adams, American, about 1757–1799, *The Independent
Chronicle and the Universal Advertiser*, 1798. Letterpress with woodcuts, 52 × 33 cm,
(20½ × 13 in.). Museum of Fine Arts, Boston. Gift of Peter Butrym, 2009.5150.
Photograph © 2016 Museum of Fine Arts, Boston.

Library of Congress Cataloging-in-Publication Data

Names: Lincoln, Benjamin, 1756–1788, author. | Mead, Philip C., editor. | Wood,
  Gordon S., editor.
Title: Essays by "The Free Republican," 1784–1786 / Benjamin Lincoln, Jr. ; edited
  and with an introduction by Philip C. Mead & Gordon S. Wood.
Description: Indianapolis : Liberty Fund, [2017] | Includes bibliographical references
  and index.
Identifiers: LCCN 2016019310| ISBN 9780865978027 (paperback : alkaline paper) |
  ISBN 9781614872764 (ePub) | ISBN 9781614879220 (PDF) | ISBN 9781614876526
  (Kindle)
Subjects: LCSH: United States—Politics and government—1783–1789—Sources. |
  Massachusetts—Politics and government—1775–1865—Sources. | United States—
  Social conditions—To 1865—Sources. | United States—Politics and government—
  Philosophy. | Republicanism—Philosophy. | Social conflict—Philosophy.
Classification: LCC E303 .L56 2017 | DDC 320.40973/09033—dc23
LC record available at https://lccn.loc.gov/2016019310

LIBERTY FUND, INC.
8335 Allison Pointe Trail, Suite 300
Indianapolis, Indiana 46250-1684

CONTENTS

Introduction / vii

Essays from
The Independent Chronicle:
and the Universal Advertiser

INTRODUCTION

These ten essays by the "Free Republican" were written by Benjamin Lincoln, Jr., son of the Revolutionary War general, Benjamin Lincoln, from Hingham, Massachusetts.[1] Lincoln was obviously a talented young man. He was born in 1756, graduated from Harvard in 1777, and by the mid-1780s was well on his way to establishing himself publicly. After clerking for three years with two important judges, he set up his law practice in 1782 in Cambridge. He had spent thirty months in Worcester studying under Judge Levi Lincoln; later he moved to Boston to study with John Lowell, one of the key figures in the Massachusetts constitutional convention of 1780 and a friend of John and Abigail Adams. At the outset of the Revolutionary War in 1775, young Lincoln had temporarily left Harvard to serve as an enlisted soldier in General John Thomas's Regiment in Roxbury. In 1777 he spent several months in Albany as medical assistant to his father, helping him recover from a leg wound received at the battle of Saratoga. The father and son were close, and in their wartime correspondence General Lincoln had encour-

1. General Benjamin Lincoln's father and grandfather were also called Benjamin Lincoln. But contemporaries were more apt to use junior and senior or military titles or geographical sites or other designations rather than roman numerals to distinguish living relatives with the same name. To complicate matters further, Lincoln, Jr., also named his first son Benjamin.

aged his son to write on political and constitutional questions, which helps account for the appearance of the young man's Free Republican essays.[2]

The publication of these essays enhanced what was already a impressive public career. By 1784 not only was Lincoln a trusted member of the Massachusetts Bar practicing before the state's court of common pleas but he had become a Freemason in a prestigious lodge. In 1785 he married Mary Otis, youngest daughter of the Revolutionary patriot, James Otis, and was moving in genteel circles with many powerful political and judicial figures, including John Lowell, Edmund Trowbridge, and other members of what the followers of Thomas Jefferson later called the "Essex Junto." By 1787, he was corresponding regularly with Washington's aide Tobias Lear and at least once with Washington himself.[3]

2. On Lincoln, Jr., see the biography of his father, David B. Mattern, *Benjamin and the American Revolution* (Columbia: University of South Carolina Press, 1995); and Conrad E. Wright, "Benjamin Lincoln, Jr.," 19, *Sibley's Harvard Graduates: 1774–1777* (Boston: Massachusetts Historical Society [hereafter MHS], forthcoming). On Lincoln's assistance to his wounded father at Albany, see Benjamin Lincoln, Jr. to Dr. J. Barker, Dec. 29, 1777, Benjamin Lincoln Papers, microfilm edition, 16 reels (Boston: MHS, 1967), reel 2. On Lincoln's transfer to the clerkship with Lowell, see Benjamin Lincoln, Jr. to Gen. Benjamin Lincoln, April 12, 1780, *ibid.,* reel 5. The father and son often discussed political questions: see especially Lincoln, Jr. to Lincoln, Sr., March 27, 1780, July 31, 1783, and August 21, 1783, and Benjamin Lincoln, Sr. to Benjamin Lincoln, Jr., July 23, 1783, *ibid.,* reel 5, reel 7, and reel 6a.

3. For Lincoln's friendship with Trowbridge and his correspondence with Lear, see Lincoln, Jr. to Lincoln, Sr., March 4, 1781, Tobias Lear to Lincoln, Jr., Feb. 26, 1787, Lincoln Papers, MHS, reel 6, reel 8. On the "Essex Junto," see David Hackett Fischer, "The Myth of the Essex

But unfortunately in January 1788, just two years after the Free Republican was published, Lincoln's promising career was cut short. He died of a sudden illness, leaving his wife Mary to raise their two infant sons. His father's shaky finances forced the sale of Lincoln's superb library that he had painstakingly acquired over the previous decade.[4] With the proceeds, Mary and the children moved to Hingham to live with her in-laws, the general and his wife.[5]

Junto," *William and Mary Quarterly*, 21 (1964), 191–235; and his *The Revolution of American Conservatism: The Federalist Party in the Era of Jeffersonian Democracy* (New York: Harper & Row, 1965). Lear in his February 26, 1787, letter to Lincoln referred to Lincoln's earlier letter to Washington. "His Excellency, so far from thinking that you took undue liberties with him in writing so fully, would, I believe, hardly have forgiven you had you done otherwise; he was anxious to hear the particulars of affairs in your quarter, and coming from you, he could rely upon the accounts. General Lincoln (whom he loves, & for whom he has felt) was undoubtedly too much engaged to write to him."

4. A broadside announced that Lincoln's books would be "Sold at Public Vendue at Russell and Clap's Auction-Room, Court-Street on Wednesday, May 7, 1788, Precisely at Ten in the Morning." *A Catalogue of Books Belonging to the Estate of the late Benjamin Lincoln, Esq., Attorney at Law* [Boston, 1788], in Houghton Library, Harvard University. Among the 120 titles were numerous law books, Hume's *Essays* and his *History of England* in 7 vols., Montesquieu's *Spirit of the Laws* and his *Persian Letters,* Rollin's *Ancient History* in 8 vols., Cicero's *Orations* in 3 vols., *The Spectator* in 8 vols., Raynal's *Indies* in 6 vols., Hooke's *Roman History* in 3 vols., and several novels, including the *Vicar of Bray, Humphry Clinker,* and *Tristram Shandy.* In addition to his own library, Lincoln was sometimes given the free use of the libraries of Chief Justice Francis Dana and Judge Edmund Trowbridge. See Lincoln, Jr., to Lincoln, Sr., March 4, 1781, Lincoln Papers, MHS, reel 6.

5. In February 1807 Mary Otis at the age of forty-three committed

Lincoln's first six essays of the Free Republican first appeared in seven monthly issues of the *Boston Magazine* throughout the year 1784.[6] Apparently the essays were so well received and considered so important that Lincoln decided that they ought to have a wider readership. This could be done by bringing them out in the popular Boston newspaper, the *Independent Chronicle.* So between November 24, 1785, and February 9, 1786, the *Independent Chronicle* republished the first six of Lincoln's essays and then subsequently published the four additional essays.

The publication of the Free Republican essays was indeed a significant intellectual event in Massachusetts politics. Benjamin Austin in his *Observations on the Pernicious Practice of the Law* (1786) immediately took on the Free Re-

---

suicide a week after her marriage to Dr. Henry Ware, Hollis Professor of Divinity at Harvard, and prior to 1805, minister of the First Church in Hingham. See the *New England Historical and Genealogical Register,* 6 (1852): 148, 78 and (1924): 300; and Wright, "Lincoln, Jr.," 19 *Sibley's Harvard Graduates: 1774–1777.*

6. In November 1783 the *Boston Magazine* was organized by a dozen Harvard graduates calling themselves the Society for Compiling a Magazine: Ministers: John Bradford (A.B. 1774), John Clarke (A.B. 1774), John Eliot (A.B. 1772), James Freeman (A.B. 1777), Simeon Howard (A.B. 1758), and Samuel Parker (A.B. 1764); Doctors: Nathaniel Walker Appleton (A.B. 1773) and Aaron Dexter (A.B. 1776); Bookseller: Benjamin Guild (A.B. 1769); Judge: Thomas Dawes (A.B. 1777), Lawyer: Benjamin Lincoln, Jr. (A.B. 1777); State clerk: George Richards Minot (A.B. 1778). See Robb K. Henderson, "Periodical Publics: Magazines and Literary Networks in Post-Revolutionary America" (Diss., University of Connecticut, 2009), 211–12. On the identification of Lincoln as the Free Republican, see *The Boston Magazine,* Vol. 1, copy in MHS, inscribed "Jas. Freeman."

publican. Austin challenged the Free Republican's contention that lawyers were a "necessary order in a republic." Austin devoted his fifty-two-page pamphlet uncovering "the many pernicious practices in the profession of the law" in order to make a case for abolishing what he believed was anything but a necessary order; in fact, he claimed, the order of lawyers was both "useless" and "dangerous." And more than a dozen years later the self-educated New England farmer William Manning in his "Key of Liberty" written in 1799 vividly recalled the significance of the Free Republican's essays, even as he passionately disagreed with them.[7]

Those essays by the Free Republican, Manning said, were the "the greatest collection of historical accounts" of the "feuds and animosities, contentions and bloodsheds that happened in the ancient republics" that he had ever encountered. By setting forth the many struggles that had taken place through history "between the Few and the Many, the patricians and plebeians, rich and poor, debtor and creditor," the writings of the Free Republican framed Manning's own thinking about society.[8]

Manning was particularly taken with Lincoln's essay Number V, which had drawn "the dividing line between the Few and Many as they apply to us in America." "Two distinct and different orders of men," the Free Republican had writ-

---

7. Honestus [Benjamin Austin], *Observations on the Pernicious Practice of the Law as Published Occasionally in the Independent Chronicle* (Boston, 1786), 3, 6; "A Laborer [William Manning], The Key of Liberty," in Michael Merrill and Sean Wilentz, eds., *The Key of Liberty: The Life and Writings of William Manning, "A Laborer," 1747–1814* (Cambridge, Mass.: Harvard University Press, 1993).

8. [Manning], Key of Liberty, 127.

ten, "seems incident to every society," and these "two contending interests," fed by a "spirit of jealousy and distrust," would always be in dispute with one another. "Whether the parties to the contests style themselves the Rich and the Poor, the Great and the Small, the High and the Low, the Elders and People, Patricians and Plebeians, Nobility and Commons, still," the Free Republican had claimed, "the source and effects of the dispute are the same."[9]

All of the Free Republican's descriptions of the two contending interests was fodder to Manning, who in 1799, writing as "a Laborer," saw himself as a spokesman for the many working plebeians struggling against the aristocratic elite of Massachusetts. Borrowing straight from young Lincoln's account of the "two general divisions" existing in all societies, which "with us . . . are described by the gentlemen and the common people," Manning concluded that the struggles in America at the end of the eighteenth century had boiled down to a conflict "between those that labor for a living and those who do not."[10]

This was a common division emerging out of the Revolution between common middling men who worked for a living and leisured gentry that ran through much of the polemics of the early Republic. Eventually this social conflict ended up, in the North at least, with the middling sort more or less coming to dominate the society and culture. Not only did most members of the emerging middle class of workers—commercial farmers, artisans, shopkeepers, clerks, teachers,

9. [Manning], Key of Liberty, 127; Free Republican, No. V, Dec. 22, 1785.

10. Free Republican, No. V, Dec. 22, 1785; [Manning], Key of Liberty, 127.

editors, petty traders, and businessmen — come to claim the title of gentlemen, rendering the traditional distinction virtually meaningless, but they turned the North into a middling society that honored labor as the supreme human activity. By contrast, southern society remained frozen in the eighteenth century. The South's leisured patrician aristocracy clung to the ancient notion that labor was mean and despicable and fit only for slaves.[11]

Although the Harvard-educated Lincoln had had no intention of supporting the arguments of the likes of Manning, nevertheless, he set forth in graphic terms the two opposing social interests that undergirded the middling assault on the leisured aristocracy that bedeviled American politics for decades. The many, said the Free Republican, were those who possessed only the rights of persons; their "subsistence is derived from their bodily labours." The few, on the other hand, were those who obtained "their riches and support, not from their own, but the labours of others." These men of property, wrote Lincoln, who certainly saw himself as one of them, were "the merchant, the physician, the lawyer and the divine, and in a word, all of every kind whose subsistence is not derived from the labours of their body." Because the few gentry derived their support from the same source, that is, the labor of others, they collaborated and supported one another. "As a union of interests is the strongest cement of friendship, we find them, not only united in publick life, but associating together in private." Since these gentlemen possessed a sense of superiority and seldom stooped except with

11. On the struggle between those who work for a living and the leisured aristocracy, see Gordon S. Wood, *The Radicalism of the American Revolution* (New York: Knopf, 1992).

reluctance, they rarely associated with the laboring many and inevitably courted the society of their own genteel kind.[12]

Since Lincoln, a full-fledged member of the gentry elite, scarcely imagined that a middling laborer like Manning might read his essays, let alone comment on them in writing, he was more frank and candid than he otherwise might have been. His arrogant tone and his presumption that social inequality was part of "the great arrangement of nature" were infuriating to the likes of Manning. Although Lincoln admitted that labor was "the sole parent of property," he turned that principle around to emphasize how dependent the many were on the property of the few. If the few had less wealth, he said, then "the labour necessary for the subsistence of the labourer" would be diminished. In effect, Lincoln saw the few in traditional terms as the necessary patrons of the many. "Were the rich not to be lavish," Montesquieu had written, "the poor would starve."[13] The leisured few, Lincoln conceded, might at first blush even be regarded as "useless, the mere drones of the hive; but it is to be remembered that we are not to quarrel with the destination of things, but must take mankind as we find them." It was because of the greed, maladies, and vices of the many that the few gentry flourished.[14]

No wonder Manning so deeply resented what he took to be the Free Republican's brazen bias in favor of the aristocratic few. The Free Republican, he said, "tries to prove that unless the Few have weight and influence in the government

12. Free Republican, No. V, Dec. 22, 1785.

13. Baron de Montesquieu, *The Spirit of the Laws* (1748), trans. by Thomas Nugent (New York: Hafner, 1962), I: book vii, sect. 4, p. 97.

14. Free Republican, No. V, Dec. 22, 1785.

according to their riches and high station in life, the government cannot be free; and he proposes great alterations in the constitution in order to better accommodate the interests of the Few." Although these sentiments — "urged in such a masterly manner just before the adoption of the federal constitution" — had continued to dominate American politics through the Washington and Adams administrations, they were, in fact, wrote Manning in 1799, "directly contrary to the principles of liberty and were no doubt written to destroy it."[15]

It was too bad, Manning noted, that the essays of the Free Republican were no longer in print; he wished they could be republished in 1799 so that the falseness of their arguments could be more fully exposed and refuted. At any rate, Manning himself was determined to prove that the Free Republican was wrong in thinking "that the destruction of free governments arises from the licentiousness of the Many or their representatives." Instead, he claimed, "their destruction always arises from the unreasonable dispositions and combinations of the Few, and the ignorance and carelessness of the Many. . . . Finding their schemes and views of interest borne down by the Many, to gain the power they cannot constitutionally obtain, the Few," wrote Manning, quoting the Free Republican directly, "endeavor to get it by cunning and corruption."[16]

Manning was not mistaken in seeing the essays by the Free Republican as original and provocative and openly partial to the rich. They directly challenged the principle of equality set forth in the Declaration of Independence, the

15. [Manning], Key of Liberty, 127.
16. [Manning], Key of Liberty, 128, 139.

principle that presumably lay at the heart of the Revolution. In fact, claimed the Free Republican, given "the various dispositions of men, the diversity of their genius, their abilities, their activity and spirit, it is impossible to conceive, that an equality should long exist among them, either, as to the extent of their property or the improvement of their minds."[17]

But Manning was mistaken in thinking that the Free Republican was simply defending the few against the many. On the contrary, Lincoln argued, perhaps with a good deal of disingenuousness, "our government will certainly cease to be free whenever the few deprive the many of their share in the administration of it. For it will then at once become an aristocracy." Although Lincoln realized that the many commoners would think that most of what he had to say "favor too much the principles of aristocracy," he wished to make clear that he feared the power of the few nearly as much as the power of the many.[18] This was the kind of deceptive self-deprecating argument the gentry sometimes used to justify their own distinctiveness and their separate representation in the upper houses of the legislatures.

Lincoln showed more of his true colors by contending that "men possessed of property are entitled to a greater share in political authority than those who are destitute of it." If this privilege were not publicly acknowledged and given institutional form, the government would never be free and long lasting. Too much "democracy" in the government would threaten the property of the few and the rich. Out of "a sense of common danger" the gentry in response were bound to come together and protect themselves. What

17. Free Republican, No. V, Dec. 22, 1785.
18. Free Republican, No. V, Dec. 22, 1785; No. X, Feb. 9, 1786.

they were unable to obtain constitutionally, they would try to acquire by deceit and venality. The rich few could never be kept down. "Power, or the ability of controlling others, ever has been, and ever will be attached to property. . . . The glare of wealth, and the splendor of its favours, will create an influence which no civil constitution can control." To Lincoln the conclusion was obvious: "Let us therefore regulate an evil we cannot prevent." Segregate the few in a separate house of the legislature.[19]

Bicameralism was the only solution. In order "to prevent the evil of usurpation on the part of either the few or the many, a due proportion of power is to be granted to each." Since "in a free government each citizen's share in political authority ought to be proportioned to his rights in society," each interest should be represented in a house of a bicameral legislature and balanced against one another, with the executive acting as the preserver of the balance. "A balance," wrote the Free Republican, "supposes three things, the two scales and the hand that holds it." That hand was the executive, who, claimed the Free Republican, ought to possess an unqualified negative over all legislation. "Superior to influence, and independent of expecting parties, he should throw his weight into either scale indifferently, as the one or the other shall preponderate."[20]

19. Free Republican, No. V, Dec. 22, 1785; No. X, Feb. 9, 1786.

20. Free Republican, No. X, Feb. 9, 1786; No. III, Dec. 8, 1785; No. IX, Jan. 26, 1786. In his *Defence of the Constitutions* Adams used the same image of scales in balance held by a third hand that Lincoln had used in the Free Republican, No. III, Dec. 8, 1785. [Adams], *Defence of the Constitutions of the United States,* in Charles F. Adams, ed., Works of John Adams (Boston, 1851), 4: 385.

What is most interesting about the essays of the Free Republican is the fact that they anticipated at many major points the arguments of John Adams's *Defence of the Constitutions of Government of the United States of America* (1787–1788). Adams wrote the three volumes of his *Defence* while serving as minister to Great Britain—a year or two after the appearance of the Free Republican in 1785–1786. In his *Defence*—that huge, jumbled conglomeration of political glosses on the single theme of balanced government— Adams emphasized the same inherent social division between the few and the many as Lincoln had, although he did not generally identify the few exclusively with property as emphatically as Lincoln did. But he did offer the same solution to the struggle by embodying these distinct and contending social interests into separate houses of a bicameral legislature, with the executive ideally having an unqualified negative over legislation and acting to preserve the balance between the two houses.

It is not that Adams was influenced in any way by Lincoln's essays. Between February 1780 and June 1787 Adams was serving abroad as peace commissioner and later as minister to Great Britain, and he may never have read the Free Republican; he certainly never mentioned the essays in his correspondence. More likely the writings of both men had common sources.[21]

It is clear that both men greatly admired the English constitution. It was "a government," said Lincoln, "in which

21. In December 1785 Adams in a letter said that young Lincoln was "personally unknown to me," but he believed that he had "an undoubted Character as a Man of Honour and abilities in his Profession" of law. JA to Elizabeth Brown, Dec. 10, 1785.

the supreme power is balanced with great wisdom, and furnished perhaps, with as effectual checks as the imperfections of human affairs will admit." Adams agreed. The English constitution, he wrote in the Defence, was "both for the adjustment of the balance and the prevention of its vibrations, the most stupendous fabric of human invention."[22]

But the English constitution that both Adams and Lincoln admired was the one interpreted by the Swiss Jean Louis De Lolme in his *La Constitution de l'Angleterre,* first published in French at Amsterdam in 1771. Montesquieu in his *Spirit of the Laws* (1748) had spent a good deal of time extolling the English constitution, but De Lolme's work was the first by a Continental European devoted entirely to the subject. The first English translation appeared in 1775, and the work went on to have multiple imprints over the succeeding decades. De Lolme fundamentally revised Montesquieu's understanding of the English constitution and helped to change the thinking of Adams, Lincoln, and many others on the nature of mixed or balanced government.[23]

Throughout the eighteenth century Englishmen had described their centuries-long history as essentially a struggle between the king and the people, between the prerogative powers of an encroaching Crown and the rights of the people defended by their representatives in the House of Commons. This ancient conflict between monarchy and

22. Free Republican, No. IV, Dec. 16, 1785; Adams, *Defence of the Constitutions of Government of the United States of America* (Philadelphia, 1787, I: 70.

23. John Louis de Lolme, *The Constitution of England; Or, an Account of the English Government* (London, 1784), ed. David Lieberman (Indianapolis: Liberty Fund, 2007).

democracy had been mediated by the aristocracy in the House of Lords acting as the holder of the scales in the marvelously balanced English constitution. In his *Spirit of the Laws* Montesquieu had accepted this conventional understanding of the English constitution and had emphasized the role of the nobility in the House of Lords in maintaining the balance between the major historic antagonists, the king and people.[24] In 1776, at the moment of constitution-making in the states, this traditional view of the balance in the English constitution was one that Adams shared.

Adams had been committed to some sort of mixed or balanced government well before the Declaration of Independence. "There are only Three simple Forms of Government," he declared in an oration delivered at Braintree in 1772, each of them undergirded by a social estate or order. When the entire ruling power was entrusted to the discretion of a single person, the government, said Adams, was called a monarchy, or the rule of one. When it was placed in the hands of "a few great, rich, wise Men," the government was an aristocracy, or the rule of the few. And when the whole power of the society was lodged with all the people, the government was termed a democracy, or the rule of the many. Each of these simple forms of government possessed a certain quality of excellence. For monarchy, it was energy; for aristocracy, it was wisdom; and for democracy, it was virtue. But Adams knew that each one of these simple forms of government, left alone, tended to run amuck and become perverted. Only by balancing and mixing all three in the government, only through the reciprocal sharing of political power by the one, the few, and the many, could the desirable quali-

24. Montesquieu, *Spirit of the Laws,* I: Book xi, sect. 6, p. 156.

ties of each be preserved and government be free. As Adams put it in 1772, "Liberty depends upon an exact Balance, a nice Counterpoise of the Powers in the state. . . . The best Governments in the World have been mixed."[25]

Adams put these ideas into his *Thoughts on Government,* which became the most important pamphlet influencing the Revolutionary state constitution makers in 1776. But the balance that Adams advocated in 1776 was more in tune with Montesquieu and the conventional understanding of the English constitution than the balance he emphasized later in his *Defence.* In 1776 Adams was most concerned with convincing his countrymen that the legislative power in their new republican governments should never rest in one assembly. "If the legislative power is wholly in one Assembly and the executive in another, or in a single person, these two powers," he warned, "will oppose and enervate upon each other, until the contest shall end in war, and the whole power, legislative and executive, be usurped by the strongest." An upper house embodying the aristocracy of the society, he concluded, would mediate this contest and bring about a proper balance.[26]

In contrast to this conventional conception of the English constitution De Lolme emphasized that the basic struggle was between the democracy and the aristocracy with the

25. Adams, Notes for an Oration at Braintree, 1772, in Lyman Butterfield et al., eds., *Diary and Autobiography of John Adams* (Cambridge: Harvard University Press, 1964), 2: 57–60.

26. Adams, *Thoughts on Government, Applicable to the Present State of the American Colonies* (1776), in Gordon S. Wood, ed., *John Adams: Revolutionary Writings, 1775–1783* (New York: Library of America, 2011), 2: 52.

crucial role in maintaining the proper balance being played by the king. This was a major innovation in thinking about the English constitution. A strong executive, said De Lolme, was the best check against the ambitions of the aristocracy, which always posed the greater threat to the stability of the constitution. Too much democracy did not lead to anarchy but to oligarchy or aristocracy. Without a powerful executive the freedom and stability of the English constitution and presumably any other balanced constitution, De Lolme concluded, could not be maintained.[27]

Both Lincoln and Adams knew De Lolme's book well. Lincoln quoted "an excellent writer on the English constitution" in his essays, and Adams in his *Defence* called it "the best defense of the political balance of three powers that was ever written."[28] The House of Commons, said Lincoln, represented personal rights of the British nation. The House of Lords composed of a body of hereditary nobility effectually represented the property of the kingdom. Thus, said Lincoln, "The lords and commons are the two scales, in equipoise." But to prevent that "insatiable thirst for power" from destroying the balance, the constitution of England had wisely placed all executive power in the king, "whose interest it is to preserve the balance." As long as the king was possessed of his constitutional authority neither the nobility nor the commons "ever attempted an immediate encroachment on the other." Ultimately, wrote Lincoln as the Free Republican, "it is not Kings or Lords that constitute tyranny, nor Senate and People that constitute Liberty; but it is that dis-

27. De Lolme, *Constitution of England,* Book II, Chaps. i–ii.
28. Free Republican, No. III, Dec. 8, 1785; Adams, *Defence of the Constitutions,* 1: 70.

tribution of political power, which give security to the rights of persons and those of property, which renders a government free, and the reverse of this despotic."[29]

But, of course, what really interested Lincoln was not the English constitution but the constitution of his state Massachusetts, "whose form bears, in many instances, a very considerable analogy to that of England, though the tenures, by which most of the officers are held, are altogether different."[30] The Massachusetts constitution of 1780 was the most important of the Revolutionary state constitutions drafted in the aftermath of the Declaration of Independence. It influenced the revisions of many other state constitutions in the late 1780s and early 1790s, and it decisively affected the framing of the national Constitution in 1787.

Unlike the earlier Revolutionary state constitutions, the Massachusetts constitution was formed by a special convention called solely for the task of constitution making, thereby creating what Thomas Jefferson called a constitution-making body that possessed a "power superior to that of the legislature." Because the earlier state constitutions had been created by ordinary law-making bodies, they were, complained Jefferson, simply an "ordinance" with "no higher authority than the other ordinances of the same session." The Massachusetts use of a special convention made the constitution something that was "unalterable by other legislatures."[31]

The Massachusetts constitution also created a govern-

29. Free Republican, No. IV, Dec. 16, 1785.

30. Free Republican, No. IV, Dec. 16, 1785.

31. Thomas Jefferson, *Notes on the State of Virginia* (1781–1782), ed. by William Peden (Chapel Hill: University of North Carolina Press, 1955), 121–25.

ment that was very different from the governments formed by the 1776 state constitutions. It provided for a bicameral legislature with a strong senate and an independent judiciary whose members served during good behavior. It also created a strong governor who was granted some of the prerogative powers that had been stripped from the executives in the state constitutions drafted in 1776. The Massachusetts constitution gave the governor a qualified veto over legislation, the authority along with the senate to appoint judges, sheriffs, and other offices.[32]

Since the political thinking of Lincoln and Adams is so similar, what can account for it? Not only did they read the same books, especially De Lolme's *Constitution of England,* but, more important, they shared in the conversations and debates surrounding the framing of the Massachusetts constitution in 1779–1780. Adams is rightly credited with writing the Massachusetts constitution of 1780, but that achievement could never have been the work of a single individual. There were discussions in Massachusetts that preceded Adams's return from Europe in the summer of 1779 that helped to shape his thinking after he arrived. Since Lincoln was part of the same circle of political movers and shakers as Adams, the discussions accompanying the framing of the state's constitution surely influenced both men. Lincoln in fact may have heard Adams talk about constitutional principles, and his essays may be in part a product of those conversations. So Adams may actually have influenced Lincoln.

32. Massachusetts Constitution of 1780, in Oscar and Mary Handlin, eds., *The Popular Sources of Political Authority: Documents on the Massachusetts Constitution of 1780* (Cambridge: Harvard University Press, 1966), 441–72.

Lincoln realized that all his emphasis on "discordant interests" in the commonwealth of Massachusetts might be too easily dismissed. "With no distinction in honors or in rank, it is generally supposed, that the old idea of the few, and the many, is unfitly applied. Placed on a common level in point of honorary distinctions, a trifling difference in the distribution of property, can never in general estimation, occasion so great a diversity in views, as to endanger the safety, or peace of the community." But such sentiments were wrong, as he had demonstrated over and over again.[33]

Lincoln certainly knew about discordant interests first-hand. From at least 1774 on, many farmers in the western counties of Massachusetts had been in a state of virtual rebellion. In Hampshire County the courts had been closed since 1774 and did not open until 1778; in Berkshire County the courts did not open until the Massachusetts constitution had gone into effect. Even after the formation of the new state constitution extralegal committees and conventions continued to protest the structure of the senate and the overwhelming hard-money interests of easterner creditors in the government.

Because Lincoln had spent over two years in Worcester he was well aware of the "grumbling, committeeing and conventing" of these western agitators. He told his father in the spring of 1779 that he thought the General Court's call for a constitutional convention was because of "an uneasiness in the Counties of Berkshire and Hampshire." By the summer he was hoping only that Massachusetts might be spared the "jars, distrust and discourse" that was convulsing the party-ridden state of Pennsylvania. Cicero had once said,

33. Free Republican, No. IX, Jan. 26, 1786.

he reminded his father, that "novelties," like Pennsylvania's unicameral legislature, "are dangerous things in a republic." He repeated the Ciceronian phrase in his Free Republican essays several years later.[34]

The bicameral legislature of the Massachusetts constitution, said Lincoln, was designed to deal with the problem of different interests. Since "men are entitled to political power, in proportion to the rights they possess at the entering into society," any constitution of a free government, Lincoln said, must recognize both the rights of persons and the rights of property. In the Massachusetts constitution the house of representatives represented the rights of persons and the senate represented the rights of property. Because all those who possessed the rights of property also possessed the rights of persons, it followed, wrote Lincoln, that the few possessed more political power than the many. Consequently, he said, "equality is not the principle of government," and certainly not the principle of the government of Massachusetts. Instead, the principle of the Massachusetts constitution was "a species of honour, or a respect for that distinction, which the constitution acknowledges to exist." In other words, because of the unequal distribution of prop-

---

34. Lincoln, Jr. to Lincoln, Sr., April 15, 1779, July 15, 1779, Lincoln Papers, MHS, reel 4, reel 5. In his July letter Lincoln also expressed concern that forming a constitution while the Massachusetts soldiers who had "suffered every hardship and braved every danger" were away fighting the British was "to deny them a voice" in the process and thus "the height of injustice." The insurgency in the west that so alarmed Lincoln in 1779 came to a head in Shays's Rebellion in 1786-1787. On Lincoln's repeating of Cicero's warning about novelties in republics, see the Free Republican, No. VII.

erty, inequality necessarily had to be the reigning principle of any free government. None of the patriots had ever been quite as blunt as Lincoln in making this point.[35]

By making property the criterion of the aristocracy and thus membership in the senate, the Massachusetts constitution makers had decisively altered the original meaning of mixed government. In 1776 the framers of the Revolutionary state constitutions had hoped that their upper houses would embody the wisdom and learning of the society. These senates, the term borrowed from ancient Rome, were a great deal smaller in size than the lower houses and were usually granted longer tenure of office, with staggered terms to lend stability to the mixed and balanced governments. The state senates, said Alexander Hamilton in 1777, were to be "to the commonwealth what ballast is to a ship."[36]

But, as David Ramsay of South Carolina pointed out, "the mode of creating two branches" that would embody different orders of men in the society proved to be "a matter of difficulty." Having the people select both houses of the legislature "out of a homogenous mass" of people was no solution, said Ramsay, for "this rather made two coordinate houses of representatives than a check on a single one, by the moderation of a select few."[37]

The framers in each state in 1776 sought different solutions to the problem. Nearly all provided for special prop-

35. Free Republican, No. V, Dec. 22, 1785.

36. Hamilton, Pay book of the State company of Artillery (1777), in Harold C. Syrett and Jacob E. Cooke, eds., *The Papers of Alexander Hamilton* (New York, 1961–1987), 1: 397.

37. David Ramsay, *The History of the American Revolution* (Philadelphia, 1789), 1: 351–52.

erty qualifications for senatorial candidates that exceeded those for candidate for the lower houses. Two states required the senatorial electorate to have more property than electors of the representatives in the lower houses, a means of distinction that James Madison believed superior to attaching property qualifications to the candidates. But the problem persisted, especially in Virginia, which had made no distinction whatsoever between the senatorial and lower house electors and candidates. The two houses of the Virginia legislature, complained Charles Lee, actually "consists of only one, for from the constitution of the Senate (as it is ridiculously called) they must be made up of the self-same clay."[38]

Everywhere American leaders wrung their hands over their inability to distinguish their senates from their houses of representatives. One solution to the problem lay in the special qualifications that most framers had provided for members of the upper houses, and it was soon exploited. Senators, William Hooper of North Carolina had said in 1776, should be "selected for their Wisdom, remarkable Integrity, or that Weight which arises from property and gives Independence and Impartiality to the human mind." Although wisdom and integrity were difficult to measure, property was not. And in property many American leaders saw a criterion by which the "senatorial part" of their society could be distinguished from ordinary people.[39]

Of course, the property that the elite invoked was not

38. Lee, quoted in Gordon S. Wood, *The Creation of the American Republic, 1776–1787* (Chapel Hill: University of North Carolina Press, 1969), 216, from which much of this discussion of state senates is drawn.

39. Hooper, quoted in Wood, *Creation of the American Republic,* 217.

modern capitalistic property; it was rather static proprietary wealth—land, bonds, rents, money out on loan—the kind of property that was the source of the gentry's independence.[40] That independence, as Josiah Quincy pointed out, really meant independence from "the fickleness and inconstancy" of the marketplace and from the vagaries of paper money and inflation. For gentlemen like Quincy, Lincoln, and Adams, paper money and modern venture capital were scarcely property at all; they could never be a source of aristocratic independence, and there was too much risk and exertion involved in acquiring that kind of property.[41]

Making proprietary property the measure of wisdom was not what most constitution makers in 1776 had expected. In his experience, said Jefferson in 1776, "Integrity" was not "the characteristic of wealth."[42] But he and other leaders were baffled by the apparent inability of the people to perceive the wise and truly talented. Lincoln himself lamented the fact that the people were not capable of choosing the proper men to fill the offices of government. If the people were learned and virtuous enough, he told his father in 1780,

40. On proprietary wealth as the source of aristocratic dominance in the eighteenth century, see George V. Taylor, "Noncapitalist Wealth and the Origins of the French Revolution," *American Historical Review*, 62 (1967), 469-96; William Doyle, *Origins of the French Revolution* (New York: Oxford University Press, 1980), 17-18; Fischer, "The Myth of the Essex Junto," *William and Mary Quarterly*, 21 (1964), 201-4. It was this precapitalist understanding of proprietary wealth—it guaranteed independence—that made sense of property qualifications for the suffrage.

41. Wood, *Radicalism of the American Revolution*, 68-69.

42. Jefferson to Edmund Pendleton, Aug. 26, 1776, in Julian P. Boyd, et al., eds., *The Papers of Thomas Jefferson* (Princeton: Princeton University Press, 1950-), 1: 508.

"a republican government might then be as convenient in practice as it is in theory."[43] But since this was not what the populace was really like, gentry like Lincoln thus were reluctantly compelled to endorse property as the best possible source of distinction for their state senates. In no state was this emphasis on property as the basis for the senate more conspicuous than in Massachusetts.

During the debate over the proposed constitution of 1778 in Massachusetts, Theophilus Parsons in the *Essex Result,* the publication of the Essex County convention, spent a great deal of time discussing the difficulty of erecting an upper house. The proposed constitution of 1778 was defective, he wrote, because it provided for the selection of the senate by all the freemen: "a trust is reposed in the people which they are unequal to." If Massachusetts wanted a proper senate containing "the greatest wisdom, firmness, consistency, and perseverance," it had to look beyond the common people. "These qualities," said Parsons, who later became chief justice of the Massachusetts Supreme Court, "will most probably be found amongst men of education and fortune," especially fortune. On behalf of the Essex Convention Parsons admitted that all men of property were not at present men of learning and wisdom, but surely, he said, it was among the wealthy that the largest number of men of education and character could be found. Hence the senate, declared the Essex convention, should represent the property of the state.[44]

43. Lincoln, Jr., to Lincoln, Sr., Sept. 14, 1780, Lincoln Papers, MHS, reel 5.

44. Parsons, *Essex Result* (1778), in Handlin, eds., *Popular Sources of Political Authority,* 349, 333–34.

Since the weakness of the senate was one of the reasons the proposed constitution of 1778 was turned down, the convention that drew up the new Massachusetts constitution in 1780 was determined to remedy this defect. Not only did the senators have special property qualifications, but representation in the senate was based on the proportion of taxes paid by each senatorial district, in other words, on the value of the land in each district. And if this were not clear enough, the convention that drew up the new constitution of 1780 explicitly spelled out the difference between the two houses. "The House of Representatives is intended as the Representatives of the Persons, and the Senate of the property of the Commonwealth."[45]

Of course, making the senate the overt representative of property severely distorted the traditional meaning of mixed government.[46] Property was no longer simply a crude measure of the best and wisest men in the society. It had become a special interest in its own right, something requiring particular protection by one of the houses of the legislature. In 1776 the Revolutionaries had drawn no sharp distinction between persons and their property, for such a division would

45. Address of the Convention, March 1780, in Handlin and Handlin, eds., *Popular Sources of Political Authority,* 437.

46. The Massachusetts constitution of 1780 had granted the senate the power to amend but not the power to initiate money bills. It soon became evident that this limitation, applied in emulation of the practice of the House of Lords, made no sense if the senate was supposed to represent the property of the state. Many pointed out the anomaly, and by the mid-1780s the senate had begun ignoring this constitutional limitation. See Robert C. Pitman, *Can the Senate of Massachusetts Originate Grants of Money?* (Boston, 1869), 6-11, located in the MHS.

have undermined their commitment to the single public interest, the *res publica*, of republicanism.

By the 1780s many Americans had abandoned that earlier republican dream of equality and were busy trying to find a way of dealing with a society that had come apart and increasingly unequal. These intense discussions and debates in Massachusetts in the late 1770s and early 1780s over the framing of a constitution appropriate to the newly appreciated inequality of American society created the climate that produced the constitutional thinking of both Lincoln and Adams.

The new Massachusetts constitution did more than recognize and represent the widening social inequalities of the society, it exacerbated them. In extralegal conventions and fiery publications the disgruntled farmers in the western counties of the state voiced their objection to the very "existence" of the senate. They had a point. Since representation in the senate was based on the proportion of taxes paid by each senatorial district, representation in the senate of the wealthier eastern counties would be substantially greater than the senatorial representation of the poorer western counties of the state. In the minds of the westerners the upper house was loaded in favor of rich easterners.[47]

Although the constitution seemed to benefit Lincoln's kind of gentry, he was no more happy with it than the angry

47. "Hampshire County Convention," *The Worcester Magazine*, I (1786), 294. On the western insurgents' objection to the senate, see Jonathan Gienapp, "'The Most Exalted Idea': The Development of Constitutional and Political Thought in Revolutionary Hampshire County, Massachusetts, 1774–1787" (Harvard University Undergraduate Thesis, 2006).

westerners. He thought the senate was deficient because it did not protect property enough. Even with senatorial representation based on the property of each district, the less well-off, he pointed out in essay No. VI, would still outnumber and could outvote the wealthy. He was equally unhappy with the fact that the governor's veto was qualified and could be overridden by two-thirds of the legislature. Like Adams, Lincoln wanted the executive to have an absolute veto over all legislation.[48]

Despite all his constitutional objections, in the end Lincoln fell back upon the major requirement for republican government that had been advocated by all the Revolutionaries in 1776. In order to support a republic, he wrote in essay Number X, "a general diffusion of *knowledge* and *virtue* are indispensable." And this was true whatever the

---

48. By 1787 many so-called aristocrats like Lincoln had become increasingly frightened by the spread of democracy in the states. Sometime in the spring of 1787 Lincoln wrote Tobias Lear, Washington's aide at Mount Vernon, urging him to heed the lessons of the Massachusetts constitution and to think in terms of strengthening government. Although Lincoln's letter on the subject does not survive, Lear's reply does, and it reveals what Lincoln was up to. Lear told Lincoln that he too was forced to "shudder" over fears of civil war breaking out in the country. "Unless, as you observe," said Lear, "some measures are pointed out and adopted to give security to property as well as persons," civil war would likely ensue. Lincoln was probably right, said Lear, to urge that "the people" must understand "they are made to be governed" and that "a government implies force and not persuasion." Yet in the end Lear felt that Lincoln's hard line wouldn't work in America. "I believe that in a country so free as this," said Lear, the people "must feel very severely before they are fully convinced of the necessity of being governed." Tobias Lear to Lincoln, June 4, 1787, Lincoln Papers, MHS, reel 8.

electoral process might be. "Without virtue no government long retained its freedom." And since virtue was not natural but had to be taught, "the first attention of a free government is to be paid to the education of youth." Whenever the people became "so deeply plunged in ignorance, or hardened in vice, as either not to know, or knowing not to choose those that are best qualified to perform the duties they are elected to discharge, . . . whenever either of these melancholy events shall take place," warned Lincoln, "liberty, with all her attendant blessings, must take her flight to some happier clime, and leave the government to anarchy and ruin!"[49]

A college like Harvard was a fine thing, but not sufficient for educating "the greater part of the community, men of small property, whose subsistence requires their and their children's utmost industry."[50] These poor and middling people needed instruction in public schools that were easily

---

49. Free Republican, No. X, Feb. 9, 1786. Lincoln had long been interested in education, especially since he had been responsible for the education of his younger brothers and sisters while his father was off fighting in the Revolutionary War. The "neglect of schools," he told his father in 1780, was "pregnant with evils of a political kind. *Learning, Virtue & Equality* among the citizens are the pillars of a republic. A neglect of schools tends to the ruin of them all so that in fact we are destroying that government we have fought & bled to erect." Lincoln, Jr., to Lincoln, Sr., April 12, 1780, Lincoln Papers, MHS, reel 5. David Hackett Fischer points out that the conservative Federalists of Essex County were also "forced to fall back on education as a means of recovering social harmony. 'The people must be *taught* to confide in and reverence their rulers,' Stephen Higginson declared. Like so many other Americans with a cause, they turned to the schools for assistance." Fischer, "The Myth of the Essex Junto," *William and Mary Quarterly*, 21 (1964), 210.

50. Free Republican, No. X, Feb. 9, 1786.

and cheaply available. All the villages, towns, parishes, and precincts ought to have schools and seminaries of instruction for all the ordinary people in the society.

It was on this matter of supporting widespread public education that the aristocratic Lincoln finally joined hands posthumously with his middling opponent William Manning—a linkage between the few and the many that has resonated through the whole of American history. In his "Key of Liberty" of 1799 Manning rightly understood that "learning and knowledge among the Many is the only support of liberty," but he was wrong in assuming that the genteel few like Lincoln were opposed to public schooling and were bent on keeping the many in ignorance and superstition. Despite all their social and intellectual differences, both Lincoln and Manning ultimately agreed on what was really essential for the sustaining of republican government.[51]

51. [Manning], Key of Liberty, 139–40.

Essays by
"The Free Republican,"
1784–1786

Boston *Independent Chronicle:
and the Universal Advertiser,*
November 24, 1785.

Mess'rs. PRINTERS,

*I have lately read in the Boston Magazine, several publica-
tions, entitled,* The Free Republican. *The subject of them is so
important as to demand the serious attention of the citizens of
Massachusetts, and it is treated by this writer with so much
ease, precision and perspicuity, that I wish much to see them
reprinted in your useful paper; in doing this you will convey
to your readers the most useful information, and will greatly
oblige a correspondent.*

THE FREE REPUBLICAN, NO. I.

The several governments of the United States of America
are, perhaps, the first in the world, whose existence com-
menced from a convention of individuals, actuated by their
understandings, to form a social compact for the security of
life and the blessings that attend it. Every nation, of which
history has furnished us with accounts, have had their constitutions established either by compulsion, conquest, acci-
dent or intrigue. Hence has arisen the great variety of forms
in which the Kingdoms of the earth have been governed,
and hence also those frequent revolutions, those internal

[3]

feuds and convulsions, which have rendered the world a continued scene of devastation and bloodshed. The kingdom of Great-Britain, whose constitution in its present form has been styled a model of perfection, in the eleventh century resembled a military, rather than a civil establishment. It was then governed by the feudal system carried to its utmost extent of severity. But the great objects, which the desire of happiness urges men to pursue, being constantly sported with by the Lord Paramount and his infamous tools, a sense of common danger uniting the views of the Lords and commons, drew forth, under the direction of the Earl of Leicester, in the reign of Henry the third, such exertions, as checked the rigor of the feudal administration; and in their consequences gave a deadly blow to that prolific parent of discords, jealousies, ignorance, usurpation, tyranny and every other species of human wretchedness. From that time, when the people, at the invitation of Leicester, urged to the measure by necessity, became a branch of the legislature, to the reign of William and Mary, the Kings, Lords and Commons were constantly struggling for power; the unequal division of which among the contending parties bringing their discordant interests into exercise, rendered the nation a constant scene of murders, dissentions and civil wars. They probably would have continued in Britain until the present day, unless the government had obtained its present state of perfection, by effecting a proper balance of power; or, unless, by a superiority of force, one of the contending parties had subdued the others, and thus rendered the government an absolute democracy, aristocracy, or monarchy. In the other nations of Europe, who were under the feudal administration, the unhappy people, after suffering the severest convulsions, have all been obliged to surrender the

[4]

dearest rights of humanity, either to the absolute controul of an hereditary nobility, or that of a monarch.

When we take a view of the several nations of Europe, examine the forms of their several governments, and the administration of them; when we read the pages of history, and learn, that both the worst and the best of them have been brought to their present state, by the destruction of millions of the human race, we cannot but be impressed with the warmest sentiments of gratitude to the Supreme Governor of the universe, that it has been our lot, peaceably to form a system of juris-prudence, on those principles of freedom and equality, the enjoyment of which whole nations have bled to obtain.

It has been said, and perhaps with truth, that all governments incline to decay, and that the most free must end in tyranny. This observation will be acknowledged to be at least founded on probability, when we contemplate the rise and fall of ancient nations, and compare them with the origin, progress, and present state of the modern. Civilization and corruption have generally been found to advance with equal steps. A nation, therefore, as it encreases with age, must increase in power of her magistrates, as the only resource for controuling the multiplied vices of the people. Hence a democracy has usually been succeeded by aristocracy, and aristocracy by a monarchy. But though it may be impossible to prevent the free republics of America from finally meeting with the fate of the other kingdoms of the earth, yet it is undoubtedly in the power of the citizens of them to place the sad catastrophe at a distance. And, if it is in their power, it would be a sacrilegious contempt of the noblest gifts of Heaven, to be inattentive to those measures, necessary to effect so great a purpose. What then is to be done? This is a question addressed to all, and to which Patriotism and Religion demand a manly and deliberate attention. Nothing is more true than that civil and religious tyranny are twin monsters; and that he who dares surrender his political liberty, dares in contempt of his God, to submit his soul to a shackle.

The inhabitants of the Commonwealth of Massachusetts, in their declaration of rights, have explicitly answered the question I have asked. They say, "a frequent recurrence to the fundamental principles of the constitution, and a constant adherence to those of piety, justice, moderation, temperance, industry, and frugality, are absolutely necessary to preserve the advantages of liberty and to maintain a free government. The people ought consequently to have a particular attention to all those principles, in the choice of their officers and representatives, and to require of their lawgivers and magistrates an exact and constant observance of them in the formation and execution of all laws necessary for the good administration of the Commonwealth."[1] If this answer is a just one, it is the indispensible duty of every citizen of a free republic, to make himself acquainted with the end and design of civil governments; the principles of the several species of them; and particularly with the nature and principles of free governments; and what measures ought to be pursued for their good administration, At a time when our Commonwealth is but in its birth, and when it ought to be guarded with peculiar attention, reflections on these sub-

---

1. A Declaration of the Rights of the Inhabitants of the Commonwealth of Massachusetts, XVIII, in Oscar and Mary Handlin, eds., *The Popular Sources of Political Authority: Documents on the Massachusetts Constitution of 1780* (Cambridge, Mass.: Harvard University Press, 1966), 446.

jects may not be uninteresting. This sentiment has induced me at this time to make some observations upon them.

Governments are divided into three species, the Republican, the Monarchical and Despotic. A Republican Government is that, in which the body, or only part of the people is possessed of the supreme power. If the Body, the government is called a Democracy, if a part, an Aristocracy; a Monarchical Government is that in which a single person governs by fixed and established laws; a Despotic, that in which a person directs every thing by his mere will and caprice. Each species of government, says the great Montesquieu, has its nature and principles; the former is "that by which it is constituted"; the latter, "that by which it is made to act."[2] The Nature of a Government is known by its form; its Principles, by comparing the end or object of all civil institutions with the means of obtaining that end, or in other words, with the nature or form of the government. This comparison or application of the end to the means, will shew the only way in which the end is to be obtained; or, which is the same, the principles of the government.

It has long since been determined by the learned and virtuous of every nation, that however different constitutions may have taken their rise, however different their forms may be, or by what means soever they may subsist, there can of right be no other object of their administration, but the good of the governed. The pride of some despotic princes have founded their right of governing, on the immediate appointment of the Great Lord of creation; and taking subterfuge behind that darling maxim of tyranny, that the King can do

2. Baron de Montesquieu, *The Spirit of the Laws* (1748), trans. by Thomas Nugent (New York: Hafner, 1962), I: book iii, sect. 1, p. 10.

no wrong, to promote their own emolument, have involved their subjects in every species of wretchedness and distress. But in this enlightened period of the world, a Divine Right to create misery, and thwart the end and design of creation, is confusion in language; the assertion of such a right is blasphemy and deserves the severest detestation. Whether, therefore, the government be a monarchy or a democracy; whether it be an aristocracy, or composed of all the laws and example of the great monarch of the Universe, binding alike the Prince and Peasant, indispensibly require of those in whose hands is its administration, to promote in every in-stance the greatest possible good of its subjects.

Creation and the government of it is perfect; because he, who administers it, is a Being of infinite wisdom, goodness and power. Destitute of either of these attributes, or were they not absolutely balanced and equal to their end, the governor and the government would be imperfect. Hence it may justly be inferred, that those, who govern their fellow mortals, to govern them with fitness, must possess not only power to pursue the best measures, but wisdom to discover, and goodness to lead to them. If the Prince be possessed of a sufficiency of power, (and without it government of no kind can exist) and be destitute of either wisdom or goodness, he is unqualified for his office. If he be ignorant, though he be good, the indiscretion of his measures may involve himself and his kingdom in ruin. If he be not ignorant, yet, should he be a bad man, with his knowledge and his power, the happiness of his subject must yield to his interest or his am-bition. From these observations it is plain, that the Prince, or those who administer a government, must have, united in them, wisdom, goodness and power, in order to effect the happiness of the subject, the great and only proper object of civil society. When a sufficiency of these is possessed both in kind and degree, the government, of what species soever it may be, is then in its utmost state of perfection.

Civil power naturally divides itself into three distinct branches, the legislative, judicial and executive. These three branches, in a state of nature, rest sovereignty in the individual. In a state of civil society, they are in most instances surrendered into the hands of the government, whose strength is ever in a ration to the individual's loss of his natural sovereignty and independence. In all governments, therefore, there must be some where a supreme, legislative, judicial and executive authority. The different manner in which this supreme authority is placed, and the different tenures by which it is held, constitutes all the variety in the forms of civil governments, that have ever made, or can make their appearance upon the theatre of the world. When this power rests in the hands of one man, independently of the people, it is called monarchy, when in the citizens at large, united by the social compact, it is stiled a democracy.

Boston *Independent Chronicle: and the Universal Advertiser,*
December 1, 1785.

❧ ☙

THE FREE REPUBLICAN, NO. II.

In my last publication I laid it down, as an uncontrovertible truth, that in every species of government, political power ought ever to be attended with political wisdom and virtue. This is necessary to the happiness of the subjects in all governments; and in republics, that partake of democracies, indispensibly so to their existence.

Political Wisdom consists in a knowledge of the nature and principles of a government, its relative interests and what institutions conduce to its safety, and the happiness of the subject. Political Virtue is a love of the government, which includes a disposition to cherish the nature of it, support its principles, and administer its laws. Political Power is that power, which in all governments is lodged some where of controlling the actions, the persons and properties of their subjects. But as power undirected by wisdom, and uncontrouled by virtue, might be an engine of promiscuous destruction, wisdom and virtue should ever be concomitants of it. Hence we find that to constitute perfection in the Monarch of the Universe, these three attributes are not only united in him, but are commensurate with each other. Infinite wisdom and infinite goodness accompany his infinite power.

This leads to some reflections interesting to a free people. First, That great power is to be conferred but on men of great wisdom and great virtue. Secondly, That whenever in a government of laws, there are not in the community a number sufficient to fill the several offices, whose wisdom and virtue are equal to the extent of their power, the principles of its existence are corrupted, and, unless the evil receive a remedy, dissolution becomes inevitable.

As political virtue is but the due direction and proper application of political wisdom, the latter must ever be precedent to the former, and associated with the very idea of government. Virtue in the political, as well as the moral world, is placed on an eminence, to which we gradually ascend, as the mind enlarges, and reason collects its power. In all political institutions therefore, policy and indeed their very being absolutely require, that the most careful attention be paid to the education of such as are to be entrusted with the civil authority. But education is not only differently applied in different governments, but varies entirely as to its genius and temper. In a monarchy every kind of political information is to be given to the Prince, and every attention paid to moulding his mind in the principles of virtue. The subjects on the other hand, should be taught to consider their monarch as the only guardian of their happiness and safety, the source of every honour and the object of entire obedience. This system of education, early adopted, excites a sense of confidence and security, together with the spirit of ambition to obtain the smiles and applause of their monarch that binds the subjects to him with ligatures of inconceivable strength. In a free republic the people, that compose it, is the monarch; or, in other words, the supreme power rests ultimately with them; hence whatever information or political virtue, is necessary to render a monarch great, and a nation happy, must in a certain degree be fixed in the minds and hearts of the people of a democracy. The only honours the citizens can of right pursue are those that result from distinguished virtue and reverence for the laws. Because, as each individual has an equal share in the sovereignty, equality constitutes the essence of the government. To give the subjects of a monarchy the same education with the citizens of a democracy, or the citizens of a democracy the same with the subjects of a monarchy would be equally preposterous, and probably occasion ruin in both. In a monarchy the art of governing without the power, and in a democracy the power of governing without art would form a spirit of vanity and pride in the former, and restlessness and jealousy in the latter, originate those discords and that spirit of faction which generally produce a civil war, and always end in tyranny.

As the spirits and principles of a democracy require, that degrees of political wisdom and virtue be diffused through the mass of the people, adequate to determining on the best interest of the community, it has generally been observed that a pure democracy can never exist. Perhaps never unless in territories of very small extent. But whether such a government ever can exist or not is not the subject of the present enquiry. This is certain, that many governments partake much of a democracy, and that the principles I have attempted to establish, if just, will apply to that species of government, though it be intermixed with aristocracy, monarchy, or both.

Antient history furnishes us with many instances of republics wherein the mass of the people have possessed a large share, though not the whole of the civil authority. The cause, progress and completion of their ruin, paint, in the most dismal colours, the evils that arise from the ignorance and follies of the people. Ignorance in politics is the parent of faction, ingratitude and perfidy. The black triumvirate must always create the severest convulsions, and finally be productive of slavery and ruin.

Carthage, until the second Punick war was governed principally by her suffetes and her Senate, which was composed of her greatest sages and most venerable men. Though an appeal lay to the people in case of division in the Senate; yet, confident of the wisdom of their Senatorial fathers, they interfered but little in the administration of government. At this time, victory constantly awaited the arms of Carthage. Her conquests had reached the very walls of Rome, when the people, grown proud by their wealth, took the civil authority upon themselves. Unprincipled and ignorant of the interests of their country, faction and cabal presided in their debates, and, led blindfold by popular leaders, they plucked from their own brows the flourishing laurel, and wreathed it around the temples of their enemy. The great Hannibal being driven into exile, and some of their best generals sacrificed to popular whims and party spirit, they became an ungoverned multitude. In this situation, the whole vengeance of Rome was collected upon their heads, and in a little time, their magnificent city was raised to the ground. It is certain, that the ruin of that mighty people was owing more to the follies and the vices of the popular branches of their government, than to the power of Rome.

Athens was more democratical than Carthage. That city was governed by her archons, her Senate, (from whom all magistrates and officers were chosen,) and by the body of the

people. In the hands of the last were all elections, to them
lay all appeals from the judgement of the magistrates, and
by them were determined the most important affairs of the
state, relating to peace or war. While the mass of the people
attended to the excellent institutions of Solon, the fame of
Athenian arms extended throughout the east. The Persian
monarch, with his millions at command, trembling on his
throne, solicited peace from that little city. But when the frequent and reiterated wars of Greece prevented an attention
to the education of the Athenian youths, discords and faction succeeded to unanimity and peace. Fickle and uncertain
as the wind, they became the sport of popular leaders, actuated in all their measures by party spirit and sinister views.
We see the people of Athens banishing the very man, who
had but a moment before received the prize of glory. On one
day, they are suing for peace, and on the next in a rage for
war. Instability, ingratitude and perfidy, become their strik-
ing characteristics. MILTIADES, who bore a most distinguished part in the famous battle at Marathon, was fined
thirty thousand crowns by this fickle and ungrateful people,
and finally died in a dungeon, merely because he mistook a
fire at a distance for a fleet superior to his own. ARISTIDES,
one of their ablest generals, who was intimately acquainted
with the laws of his country, and of such perfect integrity
as to be denominated the just, by the intrigue of Themosti-
cles suffered the ignominy of being banished by Ostracism.
On this occasion, a peasant, who could not write, and did
not know Aristides, applied to him, and desired him to put
the name of Aristides on his shell. "Has he done any wrong,
said Aristides, that you are for condemning him in this manner?" "No, replied the other, I do not so much as know him;
but I am quite tired and angry at hearing every body calling

[14]

him THE JUST." Aristides calmly took the shell, wrote his own name on it and returned it.[1] PERICLES, to divert the undeserved fury of his fellow citizens, engaged his blinded countrymen in the Peloponnesian war, which led directly to the utter ruin of Athens.

Rome, from its first existence, favoured in a very great degree of a democracy. Jealousies constantly existing between the patricians and plebeians, each were in a continual struggle for an increase of power. The institution of the Tribunes threw the balance in favour of the latter. This widened the breach and increased the faction, until the senate under Pompey, and the people under Caesar brought the long quarrel to an issue that proved the destruction of both. Dissentions never fail of rousing the ambition of private men. Caesar's publick and declared pretentions for engaging in the civil war, were to restore the tribunes and the rights of the people. But Caesar, under the mask of popular and patriotic views, enslaved his country.

Lacedaemon and Argos, represents the same wretched portrait, and establish this truth, that free governments soon sink into ruin, whenever political wisdom and virtue cease to exist in the mass of the people.[2]

Nothing is more agreeable than power to the feelings of all mankind. It constitutes so great a part of our happiness that it enters into almost every pursuit under some form or other. Hence it is sought with the greatest ardour, and when obtained guarded with inconceivable jealously and spirit. There is implanted in the bosoms of all, a most solicitous

1. The story is taken from "Aristides," in Plutarch's *Lives;* the edition used by Lincoln is unknown.

2. Lacedaemon (Sparta) and Argos were ancient Greek city-states.

fondness of superiority, while a consciousness of the reverse gives the possessor sensations of the keenest distress. This temper and disposition is the source of envy and ambition. The former ever attempts to effect a superiority by degrading others, the latter by rising above them. Men in their political relations being men still with all their infirmities about them in civil society, where different degrees of power principally constitute the different ranks and degrees of superiority, we find some anxiously bent on reducing all to a level, others on creating distinctions, and grasping the highest. In a monarchy these passions, if not duly humoured, gratified and diverted, originate rebellions. In a democracy, if not regulated by political wisdom and tempered by virtue, they break forth into faction, party spirit and dissention. To gratify their personal views, the laws are trampled on, and the constitution sported with. A tyranny of the people succeeds, which is generally concluded in that of a single person, if not in an absolute dissolution of the government by foreign force. In times of popular dissentions and the rage of faction, a public station is dangerous to a man of virtue. Hence the leaders of the people, in conjunctures like these, are generally some ambitious spirits, who, regardless of their country's welfare, with the *vox populi vox Dei* in their mouths, drive their fellow citizens to destruction, and like Caesar, rise on their ruin, and prepare the way for a Nero, a Caligula and a Domitian.

Boston *Independent Chronicle:*
and the Universal Advertiser,
December 8, 1785.

兹 芬

THE FREE REPUBLICAN, NO. III.

It is a principle well established, that the rights of persons
and those of property are the only rights which are alienable
by the laws of nature; the power of regulating the exercise
of these rights for the promotion of publick happiness, and
safety, man at entering into political society, surrenders in
every instance, either explicitly or implicitly to the supreme
power. But as the whole power of the magistrates is derived
altogether from what is surrendered by the individual, it necessarily follows that there can be no other fit object of legislation in any government, than the persons and property of
those, who compose it.

The obtaining the combined force of all to render life and
the blessings that attend it secure, from the hand of passion, avarice, cruelty or cunning, is the only motive that can
operate on the mind of man for relinquishing those powers
and personal rights, that operate in some degree as a shield
in the more defenceless state of nature, as no man can relinquish any of those rights and powers, given him by his
Maker, without receiving an equivalent; arbitrary government cannot be founded on compact. By arbitrary government is meant that in which we do not receive an equivalent
for the rights we have relinquished, or in other words, that

in which the safety of our persons and property are not abso-lutely secured. This definition of arbitrary government is the reverse of what, an excellent writer on the English constitu-tion, gives of LIBERTY: "Liberty, says that writer, consists in this, that every man while he respects the persons of others, and allows them quietly to enjoy the produce of their in-dustry, be certain himself to enjoy the produce of his own industry, and that his person be secure."[1] As this certainty cannot exist, in a political sense, without the consent of the governed to the existence of the laws, a free government may in other words be defined to be that, in which the citizens are governed by laws of their own making.

It has been observed, that there are two objects of legis-lation, persons and property. The rights of these are differ-ent, distinct and independent. Those of the former are, in many instances, possessed without any of the latter. If a man enters into society, possessed only of the rights of his per-son, and since his becoming a member of government, has made no acquisition of any other, though he may be entitled to give his voice in every law, that respects the persons, yet he cannot pretend to have any interest in one, that is to af-fect but the property of the governed. On the other hand, as those, who are holders of property, cannot be deprived of it, or have it differently modified and altered without their consent, this must be obtained, before a law, for such a pur-pose, can of right be enforced. If a majority of the people in a government, possessing a minority of the property, could controul the residue of it, property must at once be rendered

1. Jean Louis de Lolme, *The Constitution of England; Or, an Account of the English Government* (London, 1784), ed. David Lieberman (Liberty Fund, 2007), book ii, chap. v, p. 169.

insecure. And if a majority of the people should be governed by laws, made by a minority, because possessed of a majority of the property, a door would be opened for every species of oppression. Hence, to render a law valid in a free government, if it respects the persons and property of its citizens, it must have the consent of the majority both of the one and the other. From these observations it will necessarily follow, that no government can be free, whatever may be its form, where civil power is not so disposed, as that this two-fold consent should always be had to every law, that is to direct, regulate and controul the persons and properties of its citizens. A monarchy is of all governments the most arbitrary. An aristocratical government is certainly less so, but neither that is free, nor is a democracy, unless where there is equal division of property. The reason is plain. In neither of these is power so distributed and arranged, as to secure that two-fold consent, so evidently necessary to the existence of Political Liberty. That this sentiment is true, as relative to a democracy, as well as to a monarchical government or an aristocracy, may be elucidated by an example. Let us take a society composed of an hundred men, ten of whom are proprietors of all the property. If the government is a democracy the Supreme power is then placed in the whole body of the people, united by the social contract, and acting in every instance by a majority of voices. In this case it is plain, that the whole property of those, who possess it, may be taken from them against their unanimous voice, and thus rendered totally insecure; and perhaps subject to greater fluctuations, than if the government was an absolute monarchy or a compleat aristocracy. Nothing is more true, than that bodies of men are subject to all the vices follies and passions of an individual, with this difference, that while the latter generally pursues his measures with union, energy and system, the former are frequently hurried into sudden exertion by some paroxysm of zeal, the fever of parties or the rage of faction.

When the supreme power is so disposed by the constitution of the government, that no law can be made, that shall affect the persons and the properties of the governed, without the consent of each, power may be then said to be balanced between them, and while the balance is preserved the one can never encroach on the rights of the other; but if it be destroyed, whether it be done in favour of the few or the many, usurpation and tyranny immediately rear their heads, and bring dissention and civil war in their train.

It is a melancholy idea, but it is a true one, that the seeds of contest, abuses and corruption are sown in every government, at the very moment of its institution. The poor have in their own mistaken notions, every thing to gain by oppressing the rich; the rich have everything to preserve by cramping the poor and rendering them subservient to their views. These different and discordant interests have in all societies at some period or other of their being, made their appearance, and been distinguished by various rights, immunities and powers. In some governments these different rights have been settled by compact, in others by lawgivers, but in the greatest part of usurpation and power. In Athens the men of property constituted the Senate; in Rome, the body of Patricians; in France, Germany and the other Nations of Europe, the Nobility. It is a well known truth, that the present noblemen of Europe, in most instances, date the origin of their rank from feudal administration of government, in which property was the chief, if not the only source of distinction. But rank, when once obtained, is often preserved after the cause of it ceases to exist. The greatest Barons in the European nations, having at first accumulated certain dignities and power, from the extent of their possessions, soon united them to their persons; and have been generally able amid all the revolutions that have taken place since the eleventh century, to retain in a greater or less degree, a share in the administration of government. Though, in England, they are deprived in a great measure of their wealth, yet from the riches of their blood, the honours, the pomp and peculiar privileges that await them, they continue an effectual check upon that levelling spirit of the people, which is the parent of democratical tyranny.

Kings owe their origin to war. Mankind ever have been formed into different societies, differing in their interests and of course their pursuits. A knowledge of these discordant interests can never fail to create a sense of danger; and, as it [is] agreeable to principles of nature and reason, in times of difficulty and distress, to fly for assurance to a single person in preference to a multitude, every society in the early and more war-like ages of the world, was furnished with its particular leader. He led them to battle in war, and presided at their counsels in peace. Nimrod, that mighty hunter before the Lord, is I think the first king upon record.[2] Possessed of a bold and enterprising spirit, he gained the affections of the Assyrian people, formed them to the use of arms, inured them to discipline and fatigue, led them to victory and established one of the most extensive empires in the world. From him sprang the monarchs of the kingdoms of the east, who

2. Nimrod, king of Shinar, according to the book of Genesis 10:8–12 and the book of 1 Chronicles 1:10, was the son of Cush and the great-grandson of Noah and reputedly a man of power and a great hunter.

always commanded their armies in battle, rendering every political institution subservient to military views. The States of Greece, Sicily, Carthage and Rome, had at first their kings, who were officially their chief commanders in war. When the inhabitants of the north over ran Europe, and destroyed the Roman empire, the generals of their forces established themselves their kings — Warmly attached to those, who after participating their sufferings, were the authors of their glory and success, and long habited to render them implicit obedience, the people cheerfully submitted to their government in the intervals of peace. Monarchy being thus established, that species of government has continued through innumerable revolutions, in almost every nation in Europe, to the present day. In some, the power of the kings is greatly encreased, in others diminished, but in all they have invariably retained the supreme command of the armies.

Under the feudal system we find, that civil power was divided into three distinct branches. The king or lord paramount, had his share; the great barons and the people had theirs. In France and some other European governments, a variety of events have concurred to deprive the lords and Commons of their whole authority, and vested the supreme power absolutely in the monarchy. In England we find the reverse. The people have obtained their due proportion of political power, which, under the present form of their government, is so wisely distributed and equally balanced, that it is perhaps beyond the reach of human wisdom to devise a system, in which life, and the blessings of it can be more effectually secured. But if the balance should be destroyed, or in other words, if one branch of the government should ever obtain the power of either of the others, liberty would at once be banished and tyranny succeed in her place. For instance, if the people should dethrone the monarch, and usurp his authority, the rights both of persons and property would at once be afloat. If the king on the other hand, should ever wrest from the people their privileges and powers, and arrest them to himself, life and all its enjoyments would be held at the miserable tenure of an individual's will and caprice.

From the observations that have been made, if true, I think it is plain, that when power is so disposed and balanced as to render the persons and property of the governed secure, patriotism consists in endeavors to preserve the balance. Wherefore, as the balance may be destroyed, as well by the encroachments of the many on the rights of the few, as by the encroachments of the few on the rights of the many, popular leaders may not, at all times be patriots.

A balance supposes three things, the two scales and the hand that holds it. If the supreme power be altogether divided between the persons and property of the governed, though it be so distributed, that the scales shall perfectly poise, yet the experience of ages has taught us, that that government cannot long continue free. So exorbitant are the desires of men for power, that each will be grasping at the whole, and in a little time destroy the balance. In Athens the supreme power was vested in the Senate and the People, and though the execution of the laws was placed in the hands of other magistrates, yet as no checks were provided against the encroachments of the Senate on the people, or the people on the Senate, that state was constantly the sport of dissention and cabal. A few years after the institution of Solon, Pisistratus rendered himself the tyrant of the city.[3]

3. Pisistratus, tyrant who ruled in Athens during most of the years between 561 and 527 B.C.

After his decease and the expulsion of his family, the laws of Solon were again revived. But after a few years, being torn to pieces by internal feuds, their constitution was again thrown aside, and the whole administration of their affairs given to four hundred magistrates chosen by the people. But these magistrates proving a body of insupportable tyrants, they were soon deposed in rage. Thus for the want of some constitutional checks, the government of Athens was as unstable as the tempers of its inhabitants, and continued constantly fluctuating, until with all Greece, it submitted to the arms of Rome. Syracuse represents a similar picture. The supreme power of the city was placed in the hands of the elders and the people. But the latter soon destroyed the balance, murdered the best and wisest citizens, and sported away their liberty for the adulating speeches of Dionysius, who proved one of the must cruel tyrants upon record. It is also a well known truth, that the contests between the Patricians and Plebeians of Rome for that part of the supreme power, which was vested in the Tarquins, and which on their expulsion, in a sense became derelict, ended in the destruction of the balance, and the consequent ruin of that great mistress of the world.[4]

These examples and many others that might be adduced from the histories of Venice, Genoa, Holland and other European States, incontestably prove the principles of human nature to be such, that to preserve a government free, or in other words, to preserve a balance of power between the persons and properties of the governed, it is not enough to

4. The Tarquins, a Roman family that supplied some of the semi-legendary kings of Rome; their expulsion marked the beginning of the Roman Republic.

divide and balance it between them; but a certain portion of the supreme authority must be reserved and lodged in other hands, which shall be able at all times to check those encroachments, that must ever terminate in tyranny. With the means of preserving this balance of power, the constitution of England is admirably furnished. How these means are provided in that government, and how the supreme power is distributed, balanced and checked in our own, may be the subject of some future observations.

Boston *Independent Chronicle:*
and the Universal Advertiser,
December 16, 1785.

THE FREE REPUBLICAN, NO. IV.

After attempting in my last to shew what is meant by, and in what consists a balance of power, I endeavoured to prove, that political freedom is derived from it, and its continuance depends altogether on the preservation of it, If these observations have truth for their basis, it must be plain, that in order clearly to understand the principles and spirit of our own government, we must know how this balance is provided, and what checks are instituted to preserve it. When this balance and its checks are fully discovered and precisely delineated, it will be easy to discover that line of conduct and system of jurisprudence, which every patriotic citizen is indispensably bound to pursue.

Before we enter upon any observations respecting the government of the Commonwealth of Massachusetts, it may not be amiss to make a few reflections on the constitution of England, as that is a government, in which the supreme power is balanced with great wisdom, and furnished, perhaps, with as effectual checks as the imperfection of human affairs will admit. A government, which, when administered agreeably to its principles, ensures the enjoyment of as great a share of liberty and political happiness, as any one that has yet appeared in the annals of the world, The lords and com-

mons make the laws; the king holding his office by hereditary right, and independent of both branches of the legislature approves or disapproves the laws, appoints judges to
interpret them, and all the officers civil and military necessary for the execution.

The house of commons, chosen and deputed by the
people, from amongst themselves, represent the personal
rights of the nation. The house of lords, composed of a body
of hereditary nobility, formerly the immediate proprietors
of the principal part of the lands in the kingdom, and at this
day possessed in general, not only of very extensive interests, but in every instance distinguished by exclusive dignities, immunities and powers, effectually represent the property of the kingdom. For no law can be made, that shall do
an injury to the holders of property and deprive them of
any of their peculiar advantages and rights, without at once
affecting each of their lordships, in whom, are united extensive wealth and all the honours and dignities, which it
generally brings in its train. Here then we find the supreme
legislative power so divided, that no law can take place, without twofold consent of persons and property, the essence
of civil liberty. The lords and commons are the two scales,
in equipoise. But if these two bodies, in addition to their
legislative power, were vested with the judicial and executive, which include the whole that can exist in any political
institution, the histories, both of ancient and modern republics, incontestably prove, that the government could not long
continue free. That insatiable thirst for power, so natural to
the human bosom, must originate those discords and dissentions, which would destroy the balance and immediately
introduce the wretchedness of tyranny under some form
or other. When Charles was beheaded and the commons

usurped the power of the monarch, this broke the balance; and what was the consequence? The house of lords were directly voted to be dangerous and useless; the people became the unrestrained monarch of the nation, and prepared the way for the infamous despotism of a Cromwell.

To prevent these dire effects of ambition, which, in all ages, if uncontrouled, has never failed to destroy the peace and happiness of society, the constitution of England has wisely deprived the legislature of all executive power, and placed it in the hands of the king, who holds his office for life by hereditary right, and independent both of the nobility and people. The king constitutes a third branch of legislation; and as the commons have a negative on the doings of the lords, the lords on those of the commons, and the king on both, in case of a contest between either two the branches for an addition of power, there is ever a third, who is able to hold, and whose interest it is to preserve the balance. For whenever the equipoise is destroyed, all the powers of government seem necessarily to flow into the preponderating scale. Wherefore it is plain, that that very rage for power, which renders it an instrument of wretchedness and ruin, unless guarded by some effectual means of controul, becomes when these means are provided, the strongest barrier of our freedom. Civil government bears a strong analogy to the moral. The former is kept in harmony and peace by the agency of different interests, when properly directed and arranged; the blessings arising from the latter are commonly, and perhaps always, affected, by summoning up the passions, those springs of human action, and preventing the undue controul of one by checking and balancing it by the influence of the others.

In case of a contest between the king and commons it

must be the interest of the house of lords to prevent the success of either. The protectorate of Cromwell, on the one hand, and the insupportable oppressions of the first Henrys, on the other, put the truth of the position beyond the reach of dispute.

Should the King and nobility engage in a struggle for the prerogative of each other, the commons must stand in opposition to the views of both. If the nobility should prevail the government will undoubtedly become an absolute monarchy. The lesson of Thrasybulus, the tyrant of Miletos to Periander the tyrant of Corinth, ought ever to be borne in remembrance by the people of England, especially when the rights and the prerogatives of the nobility are encroached upon the influence and power of the throne. Periander asked of Thrasybulus, what measures he should take with his new acquired subjects. The latter without any other answer led the messengers into a field of wheat, where in walking along, he beat down every ear of corn that was higher than the rest.[1]

Both branches of the legislative power, being deprived of all share in the executive, it is impossible that either the lords or commons should encroach immediately on the jurisdiction of each other, but by consent or inadvertence. The former is by no means presumable. But in case that either the former or the latter should take place, the interest of the king on many accounts must be opposed to every such innovation and unconstitutional encroachment. Power always giving ardour to the spirits of men, a political body, in

1. Thrasybulus, tyrant of Miletus in the seventh century B.C., was an ally of Periander of Corinth; the anecdote about the field of wheat comes from Herodotus's *Histories*.

the undue acquisition of it, never moves, but with increasing strength and an accelerated motion. It must be opposed in the first stages of its efforts, or otherwise, though it possibly may not be able to bear down all opposition, yet it cannot fail to throw the government into convulsions, which, probably, will terminate in the accumulated horrors of a civil war. It was from this principle, that Cicero, who well knew the tempers of men and their influence on government, undertakes to assure us, "that novelties in republics are dangerous things."[2]

But I do not, at present, recollect any instances, in which, while the king was possessed of his constitutional authority, that either the nobility or commons have ever attempted an immediate encroachment on each other, tho' instances are frequent where they have endeavoured to obtain the prerogative of the monarch, in order to give efficacy to their views of destroying the balance, and thus, to effect a despotic aggrandisement of themselves. These attempts however have been generally checked without the interference of the crown.

The present claims of the House of Commons, headed by Fox, and encouraged by the young Prince of Wales, appears to me to be a subject, that ought to rouse the exertions of every friend to the constitution of England.[3] They strike

2. The exact source of the Cicero quotation is unknown, but the idea that a passion for novelties was dangerous for republics was common among the ancients.

3. Charles James Fox (1749–1806), English Whig politician, a close associate of George Augustus Frederick, the Prince of Wales; he was bitterly disliked by George III for tutoring his son in debauchery. In 1783 Fox and Lord North formed a brief ministry; although it only lasted several months, during that time Fox taunted and challenged the authority

at the very existence of monarchy. The king can act, and is accountable, but by his ministers, and if the right of controuling or even approbating his appointments is vested in the commons, the principal part of his authority vanishes in an instant. The right of approving necessarily supposes the reverse; of course if the doctrine of the commons should prevail, monarchy will only become a mere instrument in their hands, for the purpose of making such appointments as their affairs should dictate. In the time of Charles the first, the King was deprived of the right of appointing any officer of state, unless by the advice and approbation of parliament. This, says the historian, gave a most fatal blow to the regal prerogative, and in a manner dethroned the prince. Should the same event again take place, and the authority of the monarchy, as in the reign of Charles, be vested in the commons, I will venture to predict, that in a little time, some daring spirit, aided, perhaps, by foreign force, will rise a second Cromwell from the ruins of monarchy. The struggle between his majesty and the commons has exceedingly convulsed the nation, and nothing but the firmness of the king, supported by the nobility, will save the constitution from ruin. Should he persevere in his opposition with manliness and spirit, success will probably await him, unless corruption has pervaded the whole mass of the people.

It has generally been supposed that the government of England is not free, by reason of the prodigious extent of regal authority. It is true the prerogative of the king is very extensive. He appoints every officer of the kingdom, dis-

---

of George III, making clear that the ministers, not the king, ran the government. By the time Lincoln wrote his essays the ministry was headed by the younger Pitt.

solves the parliament, summons them again to existence, commands the fleets and armies, makes war and peace, negotiates treaties and holds the purse strings of the kingdom. But, though he is possessed of these powers, and many more, yet he of himself cannot prescribe a single rule of the actions of his subjects; he can only execute such as are prescribed by others. And, though it is with him to draw monies from the public treasury, yet he cannot give it supplies; and without them, his Majesty, with all powers and regal pomp about him, becomes a cypher. It is not Kings or Lords that constitute tyranny, nor Senate and People that constitute liberty; but it is that distribution of political power, which gives security to the rights of persons and those of property, which renders a government free, and the reverse of this despotic.

It is a question, that has long been the subject of speculation and conjecture, whether the government of England inclines most to a monarchy or a democracy. It has generally been supposed to incline most to the former, because of the many means, with which the king furnished, of extending his influence throughout the kingdom. But if I might be permitted to hazard my sentiments, I should readily give it as my opinion, that it inclines most to the latter. The king certainly can never become an absolute monarch, or in other words, deprive the people of all share in the administration of government, but by the exercise of great address and probably the effects of a civil war. The Commons, on the other hand, by a refusal to give supplies to the public treasury, may in effect, dethrone the monarch in a day. And if this temper and disposition should generally prevail among the mass of the people, even if the king should resort to the assistance of his armies, he yet must fall a sacrifice to popular resentment. The people of England are numerous, spirited, enterprizing and powerful. The truth of this observation is verified in almost every page of the English history. And agreeably hereto, we find, that from the first existence of the House of Commons, commencing under the Earl of Leicester, in the reign of Henry the third, they have been in a constant encrease of their authority and power. The spirit of revolution, as it gratifies the pride of such as are engaged in it, by giving importance to the most obscure, is more readily diffused than a spirit of submission. Convulsions in the political world, like those in the natural, frequently reverse the order of things and bring those into view, who would otherwise have forever remained in obscurity. When I consider these things and reflect on the extensive power that remains in the hands of the people of England it is to me a matter of some surprise that the government has not long since become a democracy.

Having made these general observations respecting the English constitution, the nature of a balance of power, and the mode in which it is provided, and preserved in that government, we pass now to some observations respecting the constitution of this Commonwealth, whose form bears, in many instances, a very considerable analogy to that of England, though the tenures, by which most of the officers are held, are altogether different.

Our House of Representatives chosen by towns, in proportion to their numbers, represent the personal rights of the Community. The Senate, chosen by Counties, in proportion to their property, represents its rights of property. These two branches, having a negative each on the other, make the laws, by which the citizens are governed; but no part of the executive authority lies with them. This is vested in the Gover-

nour, chosen annually by the People, and possessing a qualified negative on both branches of the legislature. The judicial
officers in this Commonwealth, as in England, are appointed
by the supreme executive, and as in that government, hold
their offices, in most instances, for life, determinable on
misbehaviour. In England, this misbehaviour is to be determined by the Lords on an impeachment of the commons; in
this government, by the Senate, on an impeachment of the
Representatives. As the whole executive power is vested in
the governor, had he an unqualified negative, political power
in this Commonwealth during its delegation, would be distributed nearly in the same manner as by the constitution of
England; and so long as the government should be administered agreeable to its principles, every encroachment, by one
branch on another, would be effectually prevented, and the
rights, both of persons and of property, rendered perfectly
secure. But what security have we, by our constitution, furnished as it is with these checks, that they will be properly
directed and attended to? The stability of the government
and its safety depend on the energy of the principles and
motives which shall dictate the exercise, and urge the observance of them. To determine, whether any such motives
exist, and to ascertain their origin and spirit, is an enquiry
of the highest importance; especially as the blessings of civil
government depend, in the first instance, on their existence
and the continuance of those blessings in a very great degree, or the encouragement we give them. But to discover
these principles and motives, their origin, their strength and
support, requires a more minute view of the several parts of
our constitution, their relations, their interests and depen-
dencies, than we have at this time been able to take. These
subjects therefore must be deferred to another day.

Boston *Independent Chronicle:*
and the Universal Advertiser,
December 22, 1785.

THE FREE REPUBLICAN, NO. V.

It has been observed, that the seeds of contests, abuses and corruption are sown in every government, at the very moment of its institution; and I may now add, that these dangerous evils ever arise from conceived difference of interests, and never fail immediately to make their appearance, under some form or other. That government, in which the supreme power is so distributed, as the most effectually to check their growth, is the most secure. To enquire into the source of this conceived difference of interests, the effects it has on the passions and pursuits of men, and the mode, in which the affairs of every government may be influenced by it, seems necessary, previous to making any animadversions on our own constitution, in order clearly to apprehend the dangers, to which it is exposed in common with others, and the remedies provided against them.

When we consider the various dispositions of men, the diversity of their genius, their abilities, their activity and spirit, it is impossible to conceive, that an equality should long exist amongst them, either, as to the extent of their property, or the improvement of their minds. Indeed such equality seems inconsistent with the plan and economy of things. Whoever pays the least attention to the great arrangements of nature will find variety pervades the system, and that a regular gradation, arising from mutual dependence, supports the whole. This variety and gradation is not only discoverable in the natural world at large, the animal and intelligent, but is also to be found in all societies and in every moral relation of life.

It would be not only unnecessary but impossible to enumerate all the various occupations of men in society. It is enough for our purpose to observe, that, various as the employments and pursuits of men may be, yet in all societies, states or governments, they may justly be separated into two general divisions. Of one kind are those, who cultivate the earth, manufacture the produce of it, and in fine, all such as depend on their bodily labours for subsistence and support. Of the other, are all those, who are not engaged in any exercises of this kind, but subsist and are enriched by the necessities, the follies and the vices of mankind in general, and the community in particular, in which they live. Of the latter class may, among others, be ranked those, who are supported by the income of their accumulated fortunes also merchants, physicians, lawyers and divines. The wealth of this class of men is derived principally from the labours of others. Hence the less the incomes of the rich, the profits of the merchant, the salaries of the divines, and the fees of the physician and the lawyer, the less will be the labour necessary for the subsistence of the labourer. This perhaps will appear the more plain, when we consider, that labour is the sole parent of property. A piece of crude clay, for instance, is of little or no value until it has passed through the hands of the potter. The labour, that is united to it, gives it its value, and this is ever encreased in proportion to the labour of the manufacturer. Wherefore, as the latter division of men neither cultivate the earth, nor unite the laborious exercise of their limbs to the produce of it, but still accumulate property, this property must be derived from the labours of others, and of course the less they accumulate, the more remains to the industrious labourer. Some at least of that class, who are supported from the labours of their fellow men, seem at first blush to be useless, the mere drones of the hive; but it is to be remembered that we are not to quarrel with the destination of things, but must take mankind as we find them. They ever had, and probably ever will have, their follies, their vanities, and their vices, which they will gratify, and their diseases, which must be cured. This general spirit of gratification gives riches to the merchant, the maladies of mankind to the employment of the physician, and the necessity that their follies and their vices should be checked, to the business of the lawyer and divine. Hence from the moral system of things, as far as it can be traced by observation, two distinct and different orders of men seem incident to every society, which though on the whole absolutely necessary to the happiness of each other, yet by differing in their immediate interests and pursuits, can never fail to originate that spirit of jealousy and distrust, which always proves a fruitful source of contests and dissention.

Whoever has attended to the administration of our government must have discovered the influences of this spirit of jealousy and distrust. The late law, that obliged creditors to take their debts in specific articles at an appraisement, the disputes relating to the creditors of the public, particularly those of the army, the efforts made to wipe off the public debt entirely, the resolutions of the county conventions, and many other measures that might be mentioned, have all arisen from that principle of opposition, against the interest of those, whose subsistence is derived from the labours of others. These very measures take their rise from the same sentiments and passions, which have produced the contests between the few and the many, that have occasioned the greater part of those civil wars, with the sad relation of which the histories of the antient and modern nations of the world so generally abound. Whether the parties to the contests style themselves the Rich and the Poor, the Great and the Small, the High and the Low, the Elders and People, Patricians and Plebeians, Nobility and Commons, still the source and effects of the dispute are the same.

If the sentiments I have advanced, have truth for their basis, it must be acknowledged that there are in our own government, as in all others, two distinct contending interests, that have had, still have, and probably will ever continue to have their pernicious influences, unless the dispositions of mankind are totally reversed. These are those seeds of destruction, that are implanted in government at the moment of its institution. They grow with its growth, encrease with its strength, ripen with its age, and at last terminate in its dissolution. Great care must be taken to prevent their early growth in our youthful government, or otherwise in the weakness of its infancy it may be thrown into convulsions and fall an early sacrifice to its own inattention.

I have frequently, in the course of my observations, made use of the terms, the Few and the Many, the former as descriptive of such, as possess the rights of persons and those, of property—the latter, those that possess the rights of persons only. In the latter description are included all those, whose subsistence is derived from their bodily labours; in the former such as obtain their riches and support, not from their own, but the labours of others. With men of property therefore, I rank the merchant, the physician, the lawyer and divine, and in a word, all of every kind whose subsistence is not derived from the labours of their body. I do this not because that men in the literary walks of life are possessed of accumulated property, but because, deriving their support from the same source, they must be interested with them to keep it open to their respective demands. Their joint exertions in favour of each other give them strength and stability. Hence, as a union of interests is the strongest cement of friendship, we generally find them, not only united in publick life, but associating together in private. This connexion is undoubtedly strengthened by the principles of dignity and pride. Ease and rest from labour are amongst the greatest pleasures of human life, pursued by all with inconceivable avidity, and, when attained, at once create a sense of superiority. Wherefore, as men seldom stoop but with reluctance, the wealthy for instance rarely associate with the laborious and the poor; but court the society of those, whose employments, from their not being of the laborious kind, place them on the same level. These two descriptions of men are perceived by all in every rank of life, and are universally distinguished in the common language of men. With us they are described by the gentlemen, and the common people. This distinction is general, because founded in the feelings of human nature, tho' perhaps few, even in their own imaginations have ever traced the dividing line. I believe, however, that it will always be found to be the one I have already drawn between the few and the many. Various examples that might be adduced, to prove the truth of this sentiment, I leave to the reflection of the reader.

At the time the constitution of this commonwealth was established, the distinctions I have described had long existed, and were strongly felt; for having been born and educated under a government, favouring highly of monarchical principles, the property of the citizens was very unequally accumulated, their employments exceedingly multiplied, and marked with different degrees of respectability and honour. A democracy, for this people, would therefore have been despotic, and in the course of a very few years, in all probability, have terminated in the tyranny of an individual. "It was, says the great Montesquieu, a very droll spectacle in the last century to behold the impotent efforts of the English to establish a democracy."[1] Had the inhabitants of this government attempted the same system, some modern Montesquieu would probably have drolled upon the attempt. A democratical government can never be free unless there is an equality of rights and of property among the governed; because men are entitled to political power, in proportion to the rights they possess at entering into society. Wherefore that government is as arbitrary, where there is an inequality of rights, and an unequal division of power. The proportion in either instance being destroyed, those natural rights, which it is the sole object of government to protect, must be rendered insecure, and the government of course, tyrannical. Duly to ascertain this proportion, establish and maintain it, was the great desideratum of those who accepted the important task assigned them of framing the constitution under which we live.

Two distinct and independent rights are by the constitution in the first place recognized; the rights of persons and those of property. To ensure security to each, the supreme power, or in other words the power of legislation, is divided

1. Montesquieu, *Spirit of the Laws,* I: book ii, sect. 3, p. 20.

equally between them, so that neither can act without the concurrence of the other. The senate represent the rights of property, and the house of representatives the rights of persons. And as all the different interest of the community may be ranged under one or other of these divisions, the whole are represented in one or other of the branches of legislation, or both. When I say that these distinct interests and rights are thus represented, I mean no more, than that by the principles of the constitution they are intended to be. Whether they effectually are, or are not, will be a subject of enquiry. — But to proceed.

As all those, who possess the rights of property, possess equally, and in common with every member of the community, the rights of persons, and as these distinct rights are recognized by the constitution and their preservations provided for, it follows that equality is not the principle of government, but a species of honour, or a respect for that distinction, which the constitution acknowledges to exist. If the provisions made by the constitution to give security to these distinct rights were in the first place necessary to its freedom, to support and preserve them must be the business of a patriot; while on the other hand, he who, to gain popularity, by diffusing a spirit of levelling though the community, will attempt to destroy them, is a traitor to liberty and the constitution. In a word, our government will certainly cease to be free, whenever the few deprive the many of their share in the administration of it. For it will then at once become an aristocracy. But it is equally true, that its freedom will be destroyed, whenever the former are denied a voice in the councils of the public, or as soon as their rights and their interests are borne away in the torrent of popular faction. It is the act and not the agent that constitutes tyranny.

In a state where there are persons distinguished, either by their birth, their riches or their honours, "If they were confounded with the common people says Montesquieu, and to have only the weight of a single vote, like the rest, the common liberty would be their slavery, and they would have no interest in supporting it, as most of the popular resolutions would be against them. The share they have, therefore, in the legislature, ought to be proportioned to their other advantages in the state; which happens only when they form a body which has a right to check the licentiousness of the people, as the people have a right to oppose any encroachments on theirs."[2]

2. Montesquieu, *Spirit of the Laws,* I: book xi, sect. 6, p. 155.

Boston *Independent Chronicle:*
and the Universal Advertiser,
December 29, 1785.

※ ※

THE FREE REPUBLICAN, NO. VI.

A DEMOCRATICAL government has, in the course of these papers, frequently represented and defined to be that, wherein each individual possesses an equality of power. And it has also been observed, that as men are entitled to political authority in proportion to their rights in society, wherever there is an inequality in the distribution of property, a democracy can never be free. It was from this idea I presume, that the department of legislation in this Commonwealth, was formed of two branches, a Senate, and House of Representatives, each having a negative on the other. As the former are chosen by districts, proportioned to their payment of the public taxes, no one can doubt, but that branch of legislation was intended to represent the PROPERTY of the citizens; the latter being chosen by the people, on the principle of equality, must certainly be designed for a representation of their PERSONS.[1] The necessity of such a distribution of power, in a community like this, I have already attempted to prove. I shall now proceed to enquire, whether by the Constitution of Massachusetts, there is, in fact, a representation of property, as well as the persons of its citizens.

1. Massachusetts Constitution of 1780, Chapter I, Section II, Senate.

[43]

By the constitution, the Senators are to be chosen by districts, and the number of each proportioned to its property. The House of Representatives by towns, proportioned to their numbers. The qualifications of a Senator are real estate of three hundred pounds, of personal estate of six, residence within the Commonwealth five years preceding his election, and at the time of the choice, an inhabitant of the district he may be chosen to represent. Those of a member of the House of Representatives are a freehold within the town, of one hundred pounds, or other estate of two, and one years inhabitancy. The qualifications of the electors both of the one branch and the other, are in every instance alike.

All representative bodies are but a mere epitome of the body represented, a reduction of the whole to a smaller scale, wherein all their property, rights and privileges are described. As the respective constituents of the two branches of legislation must, from the very nature of delegation, possess the same rights and powers in the administration of government, were they assembled in their own persons instead of those of their representatives, to determine the question before us, with accuracy and precision, it is important to consider, whether if the whole people were assembled for the purpose of legislation according to the spirit of the constitution, all laws that should be thus made would, from the nature and form of the assembly, have the consent of the majority of the property as well as the persons of the community. Were the whole community thus assembled, it is plain, that every law must be twice voted for before it could be legally binding, once by the whole people assembled in one body, and once by the people assembled by districts; in the latter case each district could be divided into as many classes as they respectively are entitled by the constitution to send

[44]

members to the Senate. The majority of the classes of the whole state would decide the vote in the second instance. The first assembly would undoubtedly answer to the House of Representatives, the latter to the Senate; for though the senators are required to possess a greater extent of property than the electors, yet as they are chosen by a majority of numbers who may possess a minority of the property, they depend on them for their existence, and must be supposed to pursue their wishes. From this representation it is plain, that it would not; for though the classes in each district are proportioned to its property, yet a majority of the votes in each may possess a minority of the property.

These reflections lead me to some observations on the Roman Comitia, which in their turn may throw some light on the question before us. The inhabitants of Rome, by the institutions of Romulus, were divided at first into three equal parts or tribes, and each tribe into thirty Curiae of an hundred men each.[2] To the assemblies of the people three things were committed; to create magistrates, make laws, and determine concerning any peace or war that was proposed by the king; yet in all these things the Senate's approbation was necessary. The people for many years gave their voices by Curiae, in which every private man had his vote. The majority of votes in each Curiae determined the sense of that Curiae, and what the major part of the thirty Curiae determined, was deemed the resolution of the whole assembly, which assembly was therefore called Comitia Cu-

2. Romulus in Roman mythology was a son of Mars and was one of the two founders of Rome. The comitia tributa was the assembly of the Roman republic in which plebeians and patriarchs both participated and in which votes were cast by tribe.

riata. The Senate consisting at first of an hundred men, and chosen from the body of Patricians, that is, such of the republic as had been distinguished by the King from the rest of the people, by reason of their being better born, more rich or more eminent for virtue, were not only to be judges in private causes, but to deliberate upon such public affairs as the king proposed, and to determine by the plurality of voices. Had this system of government continued, Rome might probably have remained for a long time happy. The people were the protectors of their own persons. The Senate would undoubtedly have been the guardians of property. But Servius Tullius destroyed the balance and sowed those seeds of faction and cabal that ever harassed the government in her brightest days, and finally produced her ruin.[3]

Taxes, until the reign of this prince, had hitherto been levied upon the people at so much a head, without distinction of rich or poor; but as both sorts were equally obliged to serve in the field at their own expence, it was often hard on the poorer. There was likewise this farther inconvenience in the former administration of the government. In the Curiae the rich and the poor, the patrician and plebian, were mingled without distinction, and every man's voice of equal value. As the ignoble and ignorant were the numerous, they had the greatest share in the appointment of officers, making laws and deciding on peace and war. Perceiving these inconveniences, Servius undertook to ease the poor by burthening the rich, and yet to please the latter by augmenting their power. To this end he divided the Romans into six classes. The first class consisted of those, whose estates in lands and

3. Servius Tullius, the sixth king of ancient Rome, by legend ruled from 575 to 535 B.C.

effects were worth at least an hundred thousand asses of brass. The second class comprehended those worth 75,000 asses; the third, those worth 50,000, the fourth 25,000, the fifth 12,500, the sixth included all those who had no estates at all, or were not worth so much as the soldiers of the fifth. Each of these classes were divided into a certain number of centuries, proportioned, or nearly so, to their property. These regulations being made, neither troops nor taxes were levied as formerly; but the first and richest class being more numerous in centuries than all the rest, furnished, of consequence, more men and more money for the publick service, than all the rest of the state besides. However, that ample amends might be made this class, Servius gave it, in effect, the whole authority of the state, by assembling the people in Comitia by Centuries, instead of Comitia by Curiae, for the votes of the former being reckoned by Centuries, and the rich class containing more centuries than all the other five, had consequently every thing at its own disposal.[4] The first class giving their votes first, there was rarely occasion to go so low as the fourth of a majority of votes. After this time the assemblies of the Curiae were rarely called, unless for matters of small moment.

Within the little compass of history that I have been acquainted with, I have never met with any system of jurisprudence wherein the persons and property of a community could be more completely represented than by the Comitia Curiata, and Comitia Centuriata of Rome. Had the number of centuries been exactly proportioned to the property of the

4. The comitia centuriata, traditionally thought to be founded one hundred years before the republic in c. 509 B.C., was modeled on the organization of the Roman army, but it came to be dominated by patricians.

class, a law established by each Comitia would have had that twofold consent in which consists the essence of civil liberty.

As the rights of property as well as of persons, are individual in their nature; and as, in a free government, each citizen's share in political authority ought to be proportioned to his rights in society, I know of no other way of obtaining the consent of a majority of the property, as well as the persons of the community, than an institution familiar, in kind, with that established by Servius Tullius. Our Senate and House of Representatives were undoubtedly intended to answer to the two Comitia above described. The first, like the comitia centuriata, to represent the property of the community; the last, the comitia by curiae, to represent their persons. And this by the House is completely effected; but the Senate represents neither the person of the citizens, nor their property; but only the persons of particular districts; because, tho' intended to answer to the comitia centuries, they are chosen by an assembly not of centuries, but of the curiae. That is to say, a body intended to check the encroachment of the people are chosen and appointed by the very men they are instituted to controul.

It must be acknowledged, however, that by the present system of legislation, many conveniences are felt. The result of a single assembly would probably be hasty and indigested, were there not a second to revise and controul.

Those who framed our constitution seemed to have conceived that property was attached to districts, and not to individuals, and that therefore, if a district had a number of voices in the Senate proportioned to the property within the district, the rights of property would be compleately represented, though chosen by a minority of persons possessing it. The error is too plain to need further observation.

From this mistake however, property must not only be un-represented, but as long as the present system of govern-ment remains, citizens that are possessed of equal rights may be possessed of a very unequal share of political power. For instance, it is very possible that in the course of a century the sea port towns of the Commonwealth, and those adja-cent, may pay a greater proportion of the publick taxes than the whole state besides, though their numbers may not be a third. These places then will have a right to send to the Sen-ate a majority of the whole, and as it is very probable that the majority of the voters in each district will possess a mi-nority of the property, a majority of but perhaps a third of the individuals in the government, may negative the almost unanimous voice of the whole. Hence I think it is plain, that the Senate is not only, not a representation of property, as it ought to be, in order to render the government free, but ac-cording to the present institution, is repugnant to the prin-ciples of civil liberty, which ever hold it as an indisputable truth, that an equality of rights ought ever to be attended with an equality of power. The citizens of Massachusetts are, I believe, at present, as happy as any people in the world: and whether this unequal distribution of power has, or ever will occasion any evils dangerous to the republick, is not for me to determine. It is however a very melancholy truth, that the wisest and the best governments, from the instability of human affairs, hasten rapidly to their decline. Of course, that, which in its very form carries with it the instruments of its own ruin, can never be flattered with a long period of duration.

Boston *Independent Chronicle:*
and the Universal Advertiser,
January 5, 1786.

THE FREE REPUBLICAN, NO. VII.

Having, in my last, made some observations on the Legislative branch of our government, and considered how far the two houses of legislation sail, under the present system, to furnish a representation of the property, as well as the persons of the citizens, I shall now proceed to make some reflections on that part of the constitution which creates and defines the powers of the executive. An enquiry into the nature and principles of different governments, and particularly of our own, being the sole object of these speculations, I have not, nor shall I, in future, consider any parts of the constitution other than those from which its nature and principles are to be deduced. In doing this, I shall continue to take the liberty of mentioning those instances in which, in my humble opinion, the provisions established by the constitution fail to correspond with its intentions, or are repugnant to its principles.

From what has been observed in the preceding numbers, and particularly in the last, it is evident, that the rights of property, and the rights of persons, are recognized by the constitution; and that to ensure security to each, it was plainly intended they should be distinctly represented in the Legislature. How far this intention has been carried into effect, has already been the subject of enquiry. But upon the idea that the representation was compleat, and that power was duly balanced between persons and property, or in other words, the *few* and the *many,* the next object of the constitution, seems to have been the establishment of such checks as would be able to prevent the Legislature from encroaching either on the Judicial or Executive powers, and by this means afford entire security to the persons of the citizens and their property. The sad experience of the ancient republics, and of some of the modern, undoubtedly suggested a measure of this kind. The melancholy history of their decline and fall fully evinces the justice of the sentiment, that though a government may be constituted with perfect political freedom, by having the supreme authority compleately balanced between the *few* and the *many;* yet, unless there be a power some were lodged in the community, able at all times to restrain encroachments, a thirst for domination, the strongest possible incentive to bold exertions, will originate usurpations, and plunge the government into ruin. The wise and honourable body which framed the constitution of Massachusetts, in their address to the people upon the subject of it, observe, "that the power of revising and stating objections to any bill or resolve that shall be made by the two Houses, we were of opinion, ought to be lodged in the hands of some one person, not only to preserve the laws from being unsystematical and inaccurate, but that a due balance may be preserved in the three capital powers of government."[1] The Legislative, Judicial and Executive powers, naturally

1. *An Address of the Convention, for Framing a New Constitution of Government, for the State of Massachusetts-Bay, to their Constituents* (1780), in Handlin and Handlin, eds., *Popular Sources of Political Authority,* 437.

exist in every government; and the history of the rise and fall of the empires of the world afford us ample proof, that when the same man, or body of men, enact, interpret and execute the laws, property becomes too precarious to be valuable, and a people are finally borne down with the force resulting from the union of these powers. The Governor is emphatically the representative of the whole people, being chosen not to be one town or county, but by the people at large. The following is the part of the constitution referred to in the above mentioned address. "No bill or resolve of the Senate, or House of Representatives, shall become a law, or have force as such, until it shall have been laid before the Governor for revisal; and if he, upon such revision, approve thereof, he shall signify his approbation by signing the same. But if he have any objection to the passing of such bill or re-solve, he shall return to the same, together with his objec-tions thereto in writing, to the Senate or House of Represen-tatives, in which soever the same shall have originated, who shall enter the objections sent down by the Governor at large on the records, and proceed to reconsider said bill or re-solve; but if after such reconsideration two thirds of the said Senate and House of Representatives, shall notwithstanding the said objections, agree to pass the same, it shall, together with the objections, be sent to the other branch of the Legis-lature, where it shall be reconsidered, and if approved by two-thirds of the members present, it shall have the force of a law. But in all such cases, the votes of both Houses shall be determined by yeas and nays; and the names of the persons voting for or against the bill or resolve, shall be entered on the public records of the commonwealth.

"And in order to prevent unnecessary delays, if any bill or resolve shall not be returned by the Governor within five days after it shall have been presented, the same shall have the force of a law."[2]

By this clause in the constitution, a qualified negative is given the Supreme Executive Magistrate in all bills and resolves made and passed by the Supreme Legislative; the object of which, in the language of the before mentioned address, is to preserve the laws from being unsystematical and inaccurate, and that a due balance may be kept in these capital branches of government, the Legislative, Judicial and Executive. Whatever may have been the design of those who framed our government in furnishing the Supreme Executive Magistrate with this negative, or whatever may have been their ideas as to the extent of it, this is certain, that he stands possessed of a power which in many instances may enable him inviolably to preserve the rights of persons and property. Were the two Houses therefore a compleat representation of those twofold rights and interests, which are, as has been frequently observed, the only objects of legislation, this negative in the hands of a Governor, possessed, as he ought to be, of abilities, patriotism, deliberate firmness, cool and steady independence, would operate as a barrier against the inroads of usurpation and tyranny.

The nature of a balance of power, the absolute importance of preserving it, and for this purpose the necessity of lodging some where in the community, a negative on the acts of the Legislature, having been frequently observed upon, nothing will be added further on these subjects; but the writer will now proceed to enquire —

FIRST. Whether the power vested with the Supreme Executive to negative the doings of the Supreme Legislative, is

2. Massachusetts Constitution of 1780, Chapter I, Section 1, Article II.

lodged in the hands of a Magistrate proper for the purpose? If so,

SECONDLY. Whether the power thus vested in the Supreme Executive, is calculated to produce all those beneficial political effects which might arise from a general and unqualified negative?

By the bill of rights it is declared, that all power residing originally in the people, and being derived from them, the several Magistrates and officers of government vested with authority, whether Legislative, Executive or Judicial, are their substitutes and agents.[3] Of course no officer in the government has any authority in it other than what is derived from the people, and this authority is particularly mentioned, limited and defined, by their declarations of rights and the articles of the constitution. If the Legislative power, therefore, makes a law which is contrary to the true spirit and principles of that great social compact to which they owe their political existence, it is a nullity, and the Supreme Executive, in a case of this kind, would be so far from being under any obligations to carry the same into effect, that he would be under every engagement, civil, moral, and religious, to stand firm in opposition to it. If this is true, a bill certainly ought to receive his sanction, before it acquires the force of a law and to place a negative in other hands, is re-

3. Art. V. of "A Declaration of the Rights of the Inhabitants of the Commonwealth of Massachusetts," in the Massachusetts Constitution of 1780, held that "all power residing originally in the people, and being derived from them, the several magistrates and officers of government vested with authority, whether legislative, executive, or judicial, are the substitutes and agents, and are at all times accountable to them." Handlin and Handlin, eds., *Popular Sources of Political Authority*, 443.

pugnant and incompatible with the existence of a Supreme Executive: For was this negative vested for instance, in a Court of Censors, the Supreme Executive Magistrate will not, and if Supreme, certainly cannot be obliged to execute any law which in his estimation is unconstitutional.[4] Hence, if he is subject to obligation in the business, he ceases to be Supreme, and the power must then be transferred to the Court of Censors, or the Legislature; if to the former, then the Supreme Executive possesses the negative; if to the latter, then the Legislative and Executive are united. Was the Supreme Executive in a Court of Censors no material alteration would take place in the balance of power, but many evils must necessarily arise from trusting it in the hands of a number instead of an individual; but as the tracing of these is not within my purpose, I would only observe, that it ought to be engraven on the heart of every citizen, that the exercise of tyrannical power is not confined to an individual. The Decimvirs of Rome were as arbitrary, cruel and

---

4. The censors of ancient Rome were officers responsible for administering the census, overseeing public morality, and managing aspects of government finance. The Pennsylvania Constitution of 1776 created a "Council of Censors," elected to meet every seven years, "whose duty it shall be to enquire whether the constitution has been preserved inviolate in every part; and whether the legislative and executive branches of government have performed their duty as guardians of the people, or assumed to themselves, or exercised other or greater powers than they are intitled to by the constitution." Constitution of Pennsylvania (1776), Section 47. The Pennsylvania constitution of 1776, with its unicameral legislature, its multiple-person executive, and its odd council of censors, was widely regarded by conservatives like Lincoln and Adams as an abomination; it took fourteen years of intense partisan pressure for it to be revised.

despotic, as either Nero or Domitian.[5] These observations lead to another, — that if a Supreme Executive Magistrate is appointed, a negative on the doings of the Legislative is necessarily incident to the office, and must be implied in the appointment. It certainly cannot be said to be Supreme, if he is under obligations to execute every law which may be made. He is Supreme not for the purpose of doing the mere will of the Legislature, but to carry into execution every law that is founded on the constitution. The people, when they choose their Governor, certainly do not mean to address him in a language of this kind, —

"We appoint you our Supreme Executive Magistrate, and you are to execute every law which our servants of the Legislature shall make, though they deprive us of these rights which we have solemnly declared we have not surrendered to their controul, and which by the laws of God and nature, we are forbidden to surrender." This language is too grossly unnatural and contradictory to need a comment: yet, contradictory and unnatural as it is, no other can be used, unless the Supreme Executive is furnished with a negative on the doings of the Legislature. Hence this negative must either exist, or a union of the Legislative and Executive powers take place, which union, it is on all hands conceded, would soon prove destruction of civil liberty.

---

5. The Decemviri in the ancient Roman republic were a commission of ten rulers between 452 and 449 B.C. whose increasing violence and tyranny led to their being forced from office. Nero, fifth emperor of Rome, who ruled between 54 and 68 A.D., infamously persecuted Christians and burned the city of Rome. Domitian, whose reign of terror against his enemies led to his assassination, was Roman emperor from 81 to 96 A.D.

Political freedom, however, does not consist in rendering the three capital branches of government independent of each other, but in such a distribution of power, that no law affecting the persons and property of the citizens, can have force without the consent of both — As this twofold consent, may be had where there is a union of these branches, the rendering them distinct and independent of each other, therefore, is but an expedient derived in modern times for rendering the blessings of freedom permanent and secure. While in the ancient Republics the dictates of common sense seem to have suggested the necessity of a division of power between the *few* and the *many;* yet expedients for preserving the balance unfortunately were not thought of by any of them. Athens, Carthage, Syracuse, and Rome, had all of them assemblies of the people: but the whole political power was by no means confined to them. Athens and Rome had their Senate, Carthage her Sussetes, and Syracuse her Elders.[6] The voice of these respective branches, were necessary to the establishment of a law. But all political authority, Legislative, Judicial and Executive, being ultimately placed in their hands, none was reserved to check those encroachments which constantly harassed the governments with factions and civil contests. Had those Republics been so fortunate as to have devised the wise expedient of rendering their Executive independent of their Legislative, their happiness in peace might have equalled their magnanimity in war.

6. The Sussettes were one of three councils in the government of ancient Carthage. Ancient Athens adopted a senate after falling under Roman rule. Syracuse was an ancient Greek city-state that later became part to the Roman republic.

Boston *Independent Chronicle:*
and the Universal Advertiser,
January 12, 1786.

THE FREE REPUBLICAN, NO. VIII.

Having fully considered the expediency of rendering the Executive branches of government independent of the Legislative, and, in order to keep them so, the necessity of furnishing the Supreme Executive Magistrate with a negative on the doings of the Legislature, the writer will now proceed to enquire, whether this power of negativing ought, as in England, to be absolute or limited as in Massachusetts.

To determine this question, it will be necessary to consider another. Is the power of negativing vested in the Supreme Executive of Massachusetts sufficiently extended fully to answer the ends proposed in granting it? If a limited power is adequate to the purpose, it ought not to be increased. If it is not, the Constitution is in this instance defective. To vest a Magistrate with more or less authority than is required to effect the object of his magistracy, argues equal weakness, and probably will lead to consequences alike destructive of political security. When means are fitted to their end, their result will be uniform and certain. The political architect should therefore attend to proportions, or otherwise his fabric, when exposed to the rude storms of factious parties, will inevitably fall into ruins.

The histories of the rise and fall of the empires of the

world, say the convention in their address, afford us ample proof, that when the three capital branches of political power are united in one man, or body of men, property become too precarious to be valuable, and a people are finally borne down with the force resulting from their union. Hence, say they, the power of revising and stating objections to bills was found necessary to be vested in the Governor, for the purpose of preventing that union which, in their opinions, would destroy the government. Ruinous then as this union must be, no permanent political security can be promised, unless we are guarded at every point against so sad an event. But that this is not the case is certain, as the voice of two-thirds of each branch of the Legislature is in every instance conclusive against the opposing voice of the Executive. Hence it is plain, that it is in the power of one branch of the government to effect a union of all, and thus to counteract and destroy the very principles of its existence. The independency of the Legislative and Executive powers being but thus partially secured, an opportunity is afforded to the artful and ambitious for the practice of that management and cunning which may prove ruinous to the best interests of the community.

It will probably be said in reply, that though these evils may exist in theory, yet they may never be experienced in practice, or, if they should, we had better suffer them occasionally, than run the hazard of trusting so great a power in the hands of an individual as must be necessary at all times to prevent them.

It is not within my province to determine whether any evils of this kind have yet been experienced, as I am not canvassing measures but examining principles. But that they may, and probably will be felt, is certain, since bodies of men are exposed not only to all the errors, vices and follies of individuals, but ever subject to more vehement passions and stronger prejudices. Popular assemblies, in modern as well as ancient times, give us the most unequivocal proof, that cool reflection and deliberate thinking, fall an easy sacrifice to the ardour of debate and the contests of parties. How frequently were the Athenian people forced by the eloquence of popular leaders, to trample on the best institutions of their immortal lawgivers, and sport away their dearest rights to gratify the raging passion of a moment. In the zeal of contending interests, the mere letter of the constitution will operate but as a very feeble barrier against the inroads of corruption. Though our Legislative bodies may not in every instance resemble the forms of the ancients, yet, as far forth as they are popular, the observations that reach the one, will apply to the other, differing but in their degree [*sic*]. The power of revision lodged with the Governor, may prove a check in some instances, but probably not in so many as at first blush we might be apt to imagine.

As opposition ever gives ardour to the spirits of men, the interposition of the Governor's negative, a door being still open for success, will, I predict, too frequently prove but a stimulous to greater exertion in support of the measures, which become the subject of objection. If they were the result of honest principles, and founded on serious argument, a sense of integrity, warmed with the pride of debate, will probably induce an adherence. Men of the wisest heads, and the best hearts, are subject to prejudices of this kind—prejudices, that seem to shut close the mental eye, and arm the mind against conviction. But if the measures should chance to be originated in passion or private interest, and prosecuted with zeal and party spirit, the charms of emolument, joined to the triumph of success, will unquestionably urge to the most pointed resolutions.

Such in general is the vanity of man, that instances are rare, in which he is sufficiently ingenious publickly to acknowledge an error. And I leave it with those to determine, who are better acquainted with the course of proceedings in popular assemblies, than I am, whether, when sides have been taken, it is not extremely difficult to effect an alteration of measures. If these observations are founded in truth, we must be necessarily led to conclude, that the power of negativing the bills of the Legislature, vested in the Supreme Executive, will seldom be exerted, and when exerted will but rarely prevail. It will I think be seldom exerted, since the exercise of it, by being subject to immediate opposition, places the Governor at once at the head of a party, and tends to the introduction of jealousies and discord. Should he be a good man, the situation must be painful; if a bad one much is to be dreaded, if the holding of the office be the object of his wishes.

There have been in all governments, and at all times, in their best days, as well as in their worst, men of restless spirits and deep ambition, whom the lust of power will drive to every sacrifice, to procure or retain the dignities of office. Hence the man in power in popular governments, knowing that his official existence depends on the breath of public applause, will, it is to be supposed, in general, endeavour so to direct his measures as best to secure the station he enjoys. This sentiment, in every instance of discretionary power, will naturally occasion timidity and decision. The temporizing of Magistrates is one of the greatest misfortunes of a popular government; a misfortune that admits of no cure but in rendering the mass of the people so far virtuous, and well informed, as not to be misled by passion or deceived by art. Unless this is the case, Magistrates of the greatest wisdom and integrity must either relinquish their office, or yield to the humours of their constituents. From the nature therefore of our government, even if our Executive was furnished with an unqualified negative we probably should very rarely find that energy, spirit and decision, which ever ought to mark that branch of political power. But limited as his authority now is, so many discouragements attend an attempt to prevent the establishment of measures adopted by the Legislature, that an effort for the purpose can hardly be expected. The moment a bill is negatived, every individual in the Legislature, from various principles, become warmly interested to support their principles, or gratify their passion; parties at once form, and a wide field of contention opens. The existence of parties is ever favorable to the views of the cunning and ambitious, as in the heat of contention, opportunity is afforded them of rising on the ruin of others; the more elevated station, the greater the danger. These observations, possibly, may not full apply to the present times; it is not for me to decide on this point. I may venture however to say, that when the people become more ignorant and less virtuous, we probably may experience the truth of them all. Should this melancholy period ever arrive, not only bad laws may then be instituted, but the government weakened by dissention, and the best of magistrates exposed to the assaults of the worst citizens. Such a character in the chair would, in so dangerous a station, therefore, probably only regret those evils, which he could not officially remedy. He must either do this or what in its consequences might be worse, attempt a remedy by private influence—an influence, repugnant to the constitution and abhorrent to every principle of civil liberty. The inconveniences I have enumerated would probably be remedied in whole or in part, by increasing the power of the supreme Executive, and furnishing him with an unqualified negative. Was this event to take place, by concluding all possibility of opposition, parties would seldom form, but all be induced chearfully to submit to a power, which, by being placed beyond the reach of their controul, would at once become the object of their veneration and respect.

Apprehensions of danger may possibly arise in the minds of some men, from trusting so much power in the hands of an individual. But such apprehensions cannot I think be well founded. Had he the means of injury, it is hardly presumeable he would have the will, since his interest and reputation are on the side of his duty. Annually elected to office, he is too much in the power of his constituents to be easily induced by any public act to do them wrong. He must know that their resentments may consign him at once, to the body of his fellow citizens, blast his reputation, and subject him to feel every evil he intended for them. These ideas it may be said, will prove an equal restraint on the minds of the Legislature, and prevent their adopting any measures opposed to the public interest. Observations of this kind, however specious, are by no means true. Every day's experience shews us, that bodies of men will act on principles and motives, which each individual in his private negociations, must blush to avow. The disgrace and ignominy of improper measures falling on a number, the public resentment becomes diffused, and rests lightly on all. Collected to a point, it would consign a single agent to perpetual infamy. The debt of responsibility to the public, is always increased in proportion to the share taken in the measures of it. The power of revising the doings of the Legislature, is therefore wisely lodged with an individual, in order that there should be some one in the government, on whom the eyes of the public might be fixed, as a person accountable at their tribunal, for the establishment of every measure, unconstitutional, irregular or impolitick. Give him an absolute negative, and no subterfuge will be left for excuse. He must then be vigilant, careful to know his duty, and firm in the pursuit of it; or stand exposed to the resentment and contempt of his country. Few men there are so hardened in iniquity, or dead to a sense of fame, as not to shudder at the indignant execrations of his injured fellow citizens.

Before I close my observations on the Supreme Executive, it may not be amiss to pay a little attention to the mode and plan of election. By the present system, he is chosen to office by the same persons which depute the House of Representatives, which is avowedly, that branch of the Legislature, that represents the personal rights of the community. The design of granting a negative to the Governor, among other things, is to preserve the Legislative, Executive and Judicial powers, independent of each other; this independence being necessary to the freedom of the government, which consists in the security of the rights of persons and property, derived from the representation and concurrent voice of both, in all matters that relate to them. As this is the case, the Governor ought certainly to be a representative of the whole property, as well as of the whole people.

Boston *Independent Chronicle:*
and the Universal Advertiser,
January 26, 1786.

THE FREE REPUBLICAN NO. IX.

It was observed in the close of the last publication, that the Governor ought to be a representative of the whole property, as well as the whole people. A few further observations on this point, may not be uninteresting. Chosen as he is under the present system of election, he certainly represents but the persons of the community. It is true, that by the constitution no man is eligible to the office of Supreme Executive Magistrate, unless seized of real estate within the Commonwealth, in his own right, of the value of one thousand pounds. And possibly it may be said, that this qualification will throw his interest in the scale of the holders of property. I agree that his wishes may always be in their favour, but his measures *rarely.* Owing his official existence to the voice of a majority of the persons, an opposition to their views may prove fatal to his political character, and deprive him at once of the honours and emoluments of the office. In a situation, therefore, where no constitutional support can be afforded by the possessors of property, he can hardly be supposed to check encroachments upon their rights, when the measure may terminate in his ruin.

The Convention, in their explanatory address, hold up to view, that the principal object in granting a negative to the

Governor, on the acts of the Legislature, was to prevent the laws from being unsystematical, and to preserve a balance between the three capital branches of government.[1] A very slight recurrence to first principles will shew, that the only reason which can be given, why laws should be systematical, and these capital branches of power independent, is, that the rights of persons and of property, or in other words, that the freedom of the government be rendered secure. I say no other reason can be given, since these are the only rights which are subject to the controul of civil society. Hence, if either of these rights are invaded or encroached upon, it must be the duty of the Supreme Executive to preserve them inviolate. The spirit and principles of the constitution require his steady, determinate interference, from what quarter soever the injury may arise, or in whatever mode it may be conducted. But under the present mode of appointment, a man in the chair, if upright, steady, independent principles, one who has wisdom to know his duty, and virtue enough to do it, is placed in a dangerous station. The preservation of the balance between the government, in many instances can never be effected unless by a firm, decided opposition to their unconstitutional designs. Whenever this opposition is against the popular demands, the magistrate can by no means expect a long duration of his political life. Hence in progress of time, when vice prevails, and is more in fashion, that important office will in all probability, be filled by men of cunning and mercenary spirits, who will readily coincide in views, and second any operations that may add stability to their rank, or promote their emolument.

1. An Address of the Convention, in Handlin and Handlin, eds., *Popular Sources of Political Authority,* 437.

I am sensible that there are but few, who are apprehensive of danger or difficulty, from any discordant interests existing within the Commonwealth. With no distinction in honors or in rank, it is generally supposed, that the old idea of the few, and the many, is unfitly applied. Placed on a common level in point of honorary distinctions, a trifling difference in the distribution of property, can never in general estimation, occasion so great a diversity in views, as to endanger the safety, or peace of the community. The fallacy of these sentiments, I have already attempted to shew in the course of these observations. There is, as has been already said, a difference of interests existing in all governments at the very moment of their institution; and these differing interests are those seeds of destruction which grow with their growth, encrease with their strength, ripen with their age, and end in their dissolution. In republics they may all of them be easily and directly traced to the rights of persons and of property. Their views are opposite, and unless duly humoured and gratified, and the rights themselves secured and balanced, no government can exist happy, or exist long. All those quarrels and dissentions, which, at particular periods, rendered the Roman forum a theatre of bloodshed, derived their origin from the discordant views of debtor and creditor. In the tribuneship of *Luinius* and *Sextus,* the *Lex Lexinia* was established in a *Comitia tributa,* which enacted that all sums which had been paid as interest should be deducted from the capital debt, and the residue be discharged in three years, in three equal payments.[2] It also forbid any

2. The Roman tribunes Gaius Licinius Stolo and Lucinius Sextius Lateranus urged reforms on behalf of the plebeians and in 376 B.C. were finally able to pass the Licini-Sextian legislation, or Lex Lexinia, that

Roman citizen from holding more than 500 acres of land, and whatever lands were held at that time, above that quantity, were to be taken and divided among the poorer citizens. This popular establishment threw the government at once into the severest convulsions, but which happily subsided in a few years in consequence of its disuse. An attempt afterwards made by *Tiberius Gracchus,* to renew the law and practice upon it, cost him his life, occasioned the murder of three hundred of his adherents.[3] A careful observer of the administration of our government will plainly discover the existence of the same principles and motives that gave birth to the *Lex Licinia* of Rome. The Governor ought to hold the balance; he ought to hold it with a steady hand, & duly poised. Superior to influence, and independent of expecting parties, he should throw his weight into either scale indifferently, as the one or the other shall preponderate. This never can be promised with certainty, unless the appointment of the Supreme Executive be by the voice of a majority of the property, as well as the persons of the community. I shall, probably, be told, that if this mode of election is adopted, a Governor once chosen, favouring either division of interests, may hold his office for life. This is true, provided he be so long eligible; this inconvenience, therefore, must be avoided by providing a *rotation in office.* Was this to take place, there would be but little danger of an abuse of power. Knowing that at a certain period he shall, at all events, return to a level

---

allowed plebeians to become consuls, reworked debt in favor of the debtors, and placed limits on individual landholdings.

3. Tiberius Sempronius Gracchus (c. 169–133 B.C.) was a Roman tribune whose agrarian reforms in favor of the plebeians at the expense of the patricians cost him his life.

with his fellow citizens, and feel the full operation of every improper political establishment, the public good must be his principal object. No inducement will be left for the exercise of those cunning arts and practices which, under a different plan, might be practised to retain the high pleasures and emoluments of power. These observations apply, with equal force, to our Supreme Executive, under our present system of election. Had a rotation in office been provided, much more energy and decision would, in my opinion, have marked the measures of the public.

If the sentiments and principles which have been offered, relative to the Executive branch of our government, have their foundation in truth, I think it will be conceded that our constitution should, if possible, be amended. But whether my sentiments are just, or, if so, whether the nature of a free government will admit of alterations in ours, I shall take the liberty to leave to the decision of wiser heads, and proceed to a few reflections on the Judicial authority, which is the only branch of political that remains to be the subject of observation.

To the end that the government of this Commonwealth be a government of laws and not of men, the Bill of Rights provides that the three capital departments of it shall be vested in distinct and different bodies of men, absolutely independent of, and unconnected with each other.[4] The business of the judicial is the regulation of trials, and the interpretation of the law.

The three prime branches of government being thus in-

4. A Declaration of the Rights of the Inhabitants of the Commonwealth of Massachusetts, XVIII, in Handlin and Handlin, eds., *Popular Sources of Political Authority,* 446.

dependent, each must be Supreme, and their respective acts and decisions alike binding on the other department of power and the individuals of the community; and for which acts and decision, neither is accountable to the others, but to the high tribunal of the people only, from whom is derived the whole authority exerciseable in a government of laws.

By our constitution, the Judges, or in other words, the Interpreters of the Law, receive their appointment from the Supreme Executive, with the advice of Council, and hold their office during good behaviour.[5] In case of malfeasance, they are to be tried by the Senate on an impeachment by the House of Representatives. There are various Judicial Courts within the commonwealth; but the doings and decisions of all, either by appeals or writs of error, are finally revised, settled and adjudged by a Supreme Judicial; the Justices of which, are supported by fixed and permanent salaries established by law. Certain of an honourable subsistence, and removeable at the will of no one, the independency of that branch of authority is rendered as secure, perhaps, as the nature and principles of a popular government will admit.

It may be said, that the Judiciary officers being exposed to impeachment by one branch of the legislature, and triable by the other, may possibly tend to destroy their independency. This undoubtedly is true; and had the people appointed another tribunal, distinct from either branch of authority, this might have rendered the Judicial more independent of the legislature; but this tribunal would soon be able to create an influence that must prove highly dangerous to the community, and promotive of much deeper mischiefs that may be expected to accrue from the judicial jurisdiction

5. Massachusetts Constitution of 1780, Chapter III, Judiciary Power.

which is vested in the Senate. On this account, therefore, and on others which might be mentioned, the independency of the Judiciary power seems to me to be as well secured as the nature of our government will admit.

The judicial being one of the Supreme independent branches of government, it may be asked why the appointment of them was not reserved to the collective body of the people? The reason is plain. It would be impossible for them to exercise it with any degree of safety to themselves, since they could never be acquainted with all the various characters suitable to the employment, and of course would be subject to ruinous impositions. Indeed the business is of such a nature, that it could never be transacted but by a person or persons delegated for the purpose. It is wisely trusted to the care of an individual, as by this measure the public know on whom to fix their resentment, in case of a wanton or injudicious exercise of this high and interesting authority [*sic*].

It may not, however, be improper to observe, that the power of appointing the Judicial officers is by no means necessary to the Supreme Executive. The balance of power, and the principles of the constitution, would have been as well preserved, had this authority been lodged in the hands of a Magistrate delegated for that purpose only; but a needless multiplication of officers ought ever to be avoided. This important trust, therefore, is well lodged in the person of the Supreme Executive.

Having made these observations relative to the appointment of the judicial department, the extent of its powers become the next subject of attention. The regulation of trials, the interpretation of the law, and the administration of justice, are the great objects of its charge.

A statute must, in the nature of things, be expressed in

general terms. To explain these, and to apply them to all the various cases that may take place in society, is the duty of the Judge. These explanatory comments are in our government, and must be in every free republic as binding on the citizens as the statute itself, since the explanation of the law is as much a part of it as if the whole had been spread upon paper at the time of its enaction; so that the Supreme Judicial Court, of a free government, when once it has interpreted a law, can never contradict the explanation it has made. This can be done, but by a solemn act of legislation. The obligatory force of a statute is derived from its meaning, and not from its letter. The interpretation of the Judge is the meaning not of the Judge, but of the law. If the law is wrong, the Legislator only can alter it. These observations, while they shew at once how indispensible it is to the freedom and happiness of government, that the Judge should be independent of the legislator, tend to explain the occasion of the prolixity of our laws. This is complained of as an evil; but in order to avoid it, we must renounce the blessings of civil liberty. That government is very emphatically a despotism where the will of the judge is at all times the interpretation of the law.

The judicial power is a sure criterion of the goodness of a government. The moment it becomes corrupt, the streams of justice are poisoned, individuals are involved in immediate distress, all private confidence is must soon be lost, and the best formed government plunged into anarchy and bloodshed. In a government like ours, it will be difficult for the legislature to destroy, at once, the whole body of jurisprudence by which life, liberty and property are secure. The Executive can never do it but by force; but the Judicial, under the forms of justice, and the ceremonies of law, may deprive the citizens of their most valuable possessions, secure from punishment, and even from discovery. With bad legislators, and good judges, the progress of ruin must be slow, arduous to effect, and exposed to immediate detection and instant opposition.

In the ancient republics, particularly in Athens, Sparta and Rome, the Judicial power was a mere instrument of tyranny. The mode of making as well as interpreting the laws, gave every opportunity for corruption. A want of uniformity and system put it into the power of the Judge of binding them to his pleasure. In England, and in this Commonwealth, the municipal institutions are so fixed and determinate, that it must be difficult for the Judicial authority to trample upon them with impunity. It may not, however, be improper to observe, that if the science of the law was confined to the Judge, he might convert it to the most destructive purposes, in so covered a manner, as to place him beyond the reach of discovery. — Wherefore, as the science of the law is intricate and perplexing, and cannot be obtained but by long and steady application, possessors and practisers of it, seem a necessary order in a free republic.

Boston *Independent Chronicle:*
and the Universal Advertiser,
February 9, 1786.

❧ ❧

THE FREE REPUBLICAN, NO. X.

From the observations which have been made in the course
of these papers, I think it is evident, that the rights of persons and of property are distinctly recognized by our constitution; and that the security of each being necessary to civil
liberty, is intended to be provided for and effected. How far
these rights are in fact secured, has already been the subject
of enquiry.

I shall, probably, be told by many, that the sentiments
I have advanced favor too much of the principles of aristocracy. An objection of this kind, however well founded
it may seem at first blush, will, I flatter myself, on careful
enquiry, appear to be altogether erroneous. My object has
been to prove that no government can be free, where civil
power is not proportioned to the rights of individuals, and
consequently that men possessed of property are entitled to
a greater share in political authority than those who are destitute of it. I was induced to this, from a full belief that a government in which this proportion is altogether unattended
to, can never be promised with great length of duration.

As property, from the principles of self preservation, is
pursued by every one with the greatest ardour and attention,
and when acquired, is at all times guarded with inconceiv-

able jealousy and spirit, its security must, in the minds of all men, be ranked among the first objects of civil society. If this is insecure in fact, or is in the imagination of its possessors subject to the absolute controul of others, a sense of common danger will, in a government partaking of a democracy, at once unite the possessors in a similarity of views. To effect their security, the power they cannot constitutionally obtain, they will endeavour to acquire by cunning and corruption; conscious, at the same time, that usurpations once began, the safety of usurper consists but in grasping the while, no limits will be known to their ambition while any thing remains to be obtained. The people, of course, must be borne down by the hand of arbitrary power, or arm in their defence. In either of which very solemn alternatives, the events of history abundantly assure us, that liberty must sink in the struggle. It has generally happened that some daring spirit, some Pompey or Caesar, have led the contending parties to bloodshed and battle, commanding but to enslave.[1]

When the whole legislative power of Rome was vested in a *comitia* by *centuries,* the people feeling their own insecurity, and daily exposed to insults, cruelty and oppression, flew to the *mons sacer* for protection.[2] There they effected

1. Gnaeus Pompeius Magnus (Pompey) (106–48 B.C.) and Gaius Julius Caesar (100–44 B.C.) were leaders of the Roman army who established the first Triumvirate as the preeminent ruling authority in the republic. After defeating Pompey in battle, Caesar became dictator and was ultimately assassinated.

2. Mons Sacer was a hill near Rome where in 494 B.C. the plebeians fled during a conflict with the patricians and negotiated the creation of the tribunes. The comitia tributia, the assembly representing plebeians by tribes, grew in constitutional authority during the following decades and in 471 B.C. won the right to choose the tribunes.

an establishment of the Tribunes, who, in the course of a
few years, introduced a *comitia* by *tribes*. This new system
of legislation rendering that of the centuries insignificant
and useless, cast the balance in favour of the people. The
people, in their turn, practising the most abusive impositions upon the wealthy, subjecting them to punishments in
the most capricious manner, and wantonly exposing them to
obloquy, indignation and contempt, they, with the Senate at
their head, long leagued for defence, rushed armed into the
forum, where they fell furiously on that renowned popular
leader Tiberius Gracchus, and having slain him and three
hundred of his adherents, they cast their bodies into the
Tiber. This commotion shook the state to its foundations,
and by introducing arms and bloodshed into the assemblies
of the people, precluded those successive tragedies, the
final catastrophe of which was the utter ruin of Roman liberty. That venerable mistress of the world, at every stage and
period of her existence, has taught mankind this serious lesson, that a government but half free is constantly exposed to
the wretchedness of civil discords and political convulsions.

In a monarchy or an aristocracy, where the body of the
people are deprived of all power in the administration of
government, combinations are easily prevented, and may
always be destroyed at the very moment of their birth.-
Though power is easily usurped where any is possessed, yet
few have ever grasped it when destitute of all. In every government, therefore, that partakes of a democracy to prevent
the evils of usurpation on the part of either the few or the
many, a due proportion of power is to be granted to each.
When this is the case, a sense of danger, the strongest of
human impressions, never exciting a wish to encroach, the
government must be zealously supported by all, from the

same principles that that in which power is unequally distributed, will ever be subject to discords, party spirit, faction and tyranny.

I will subjoin but one idea farther to shew the necessity of proportioning power to the rights of individuals. Power, or the ability of controuling others, ever has been, and ever will be attached to property. The necessities of men, their follies and vices, render them blind to the failings, and servile to the views of the rich. The glare of wealth, and the splendor of its favours, will create an influence which no civil institution can controul. This influence in a government where each citizen has an equality of power, is totally repugnant to its principles, and must be productive of its ruin. Let us therefore regulate an evil we cannot prevent. Let us attach that power to property which it will inevitably possess; and possessed by usurpation must occasion the most pernicious effects. By this means, the rights of the rich will be ascertained, clearly understood, and of course they will be less likely to be dangerous. Secure as to their privileges, all violent measures on their part, for maintaining them, will be prevented; and they will never combine with vehemence when they know they are not in danger.

In fine, a popular government can never exist long, unless the interests of the citizens are united to support it; this union of interests must arise but from a consciousness of security which can never take place, unless each individual's share of political authority is proportioned to the rights he enjoys.

The mode of the election and appointment of the prime branches of our government, the nature and extent of their powers, and the tenure of their offices having in these papers been enquired into, I have reached the end of my subject.

But before it is closed, it may not be impertinent to remark, that as our government is administered by magistrates delegated from the body of the citizens, united by the social compact, and constituting the Republic, a general diffusion of *knowledge* and *virtue* are indispensible to its support. This is equally true, whether the magistrates are appointed by an assembly of the people, in which each man's voice is of equal value, or by an assembly of classes, in which each individual's power shall be proportionate to his property, or by the concurrent voice of both. Without virtue no government ever long retained its freedom. Such an event being repugnant to the nature of things, must at all times be impossible. But the blessings of virtue must arise from a enlightened understanding, and a judgment well informed. She never finds an home in an untutored mind. The natural vehemence of the animal passions, unless subjected to the controul of our reason, necessarily hurries to instant gratification, and consequent distress and ruin. As the rational powers therefore, are to lead the way, and guide our steps in the paths of virtue, the first attention of a free government is to be paid to the education of youth. What truth can be paid to the education of youth. What truth can be more obvious than that whenever we arrive to so low a point of depravation, that there cannot be found in the community, a number of sufficient wisdom and integrity to fill the many important offices of government; or whenever our fellow citizens are so deeply plunged in ignorance, or hardened in vice, as either not to know, or knowing not to choose those that are the best qualified to perform the duties they are elected to discharge, I say what truth can be more obvious, that whenever either of these melancholy events shall take place, liberty, with all her attendant blessings, must take her flight to some happier clime, and leave the government to anarchy and ruin! What arm can save us! Without immediate inspiration from Heaven, it would be as impossible to preserve our freedom, as to convert the midnight darkness into the full blaze of day.

The Convention who formed the Constitution, fully sensible that wisdom and knowledge, as well as virtue, should be generally diffused as among the body of the people, in order to preserve their rights and liberties, have made the establishment of the University at Cambridge, and the encouragement of literature, a part of that great compact of civil government under which we live. It is enjoined upon the legislative body, and it is their duty to cherish the interests of literature, and all seminaries of them, especially the University just mentioned, public schools and grammar schools in the towns. Universities and public academies are certainly indispensible to literary improvement, and greatly promotive of the public weal; but were no other institutions formed, learning would necessarily be confined to the wealthy and the great. Town schools and private seminaries of instruction are the only means, by which the general diffusion of knowledge can be effected. They ought therefore to be cherished as the principal security of the people's rights. Their institution is but of little consequence to men of wealth, but as their interest is connected with the general good. Their children may be sent abroad for their education without inconvenience. But the greater part of the community, men of small property, whose subsistence requires their and their children's utmost industry, are denied advantages of this kind. Instruction must be easily and cheaply obtained, or they can never enjoy the advantages of it. Of consequence, unless this is the case, the great body of the people must in a few years become ignorant, servile, vicious, incapable of freedom, and the ready instruments of their own slavery. Schools and a free press, are a poor man's greatest safety. But without the former, the latter would be a very unessential provision. The people of Rome, aware of danger from the wealthy, and the great instituted the tribunitial power for their defence, and to interpose in all grievances and impositions that might be practiced upon them. But these tribunes soon forsook the interests of their constituents, mounted into power, and became the ready associates of the very men they were appointed to controul. The establishment of our schools, enables every man to be his own tribune, and to guard his own rights. The people of Rome were so jealous of injury and so fully persuaded of the necessity of being constantly in defence,—that they enacted a law, by which provision was made, that he who offered the least violence to a tribune, was declared accursed, and his effects confiscated to the Goddess Ceres: and he might be slain without any previous form of process.[3]

Schools and seminaries of instruction, throughout our several villages, towns, parishes and precincts, being of as high importance to us, as the tribuneship to the Roman people, should be guarded by all, but by the poor in particular, with as much ardour, spirit and attention. Though similar laws would be dangerous, and ought never to be instituted, yet it is to be wished that an attempt to discourage, interrupt or prevent the establishment of schools, might be considered as a crime of the first magnitude, traitorous to liberty, and the principles of the Constitution.

3. The Goddess Ceres in Roman mythology was the goddess of agriculture.

INDEX

This book is set in Bulmer,
a transitional typeface designed by William Martin
in 1792 and redrawn in 1928 by Morris Fuller Benton.
Martin had worked with John Baskerville, and his type shows
Baskerville's influence in its vertical axes, moderate contrast
between thick and thin strokes, and well-defined serifs.
The type was first used for the folio edition of the
works of Shakespeare published by William Bulmer's
Shakespeare Press.

Printed on paper that is acid-free and meets the requirements
of the American National Standard for Permanence of Paper
for Printed Library Materials, z39.48-1992. ∞

Book design by Richard Hendel
Typography by Tseng Information Systems, Inc.
Printed and bound by Worzalla Publishing Co.,
Stevens Point, Wisconsin